Understanding Yourself
Through Birth Order

By Clifford E. Isaacson

Published by the Upper Des Moines
Counseling Center, Inc.
Algona, Iowa 50511

Printed in the United States of America

Library of Congress
Cataloging-in-Publication Data

Isaacson, Clifford E., 1934—
    Understanding Yourself Through Birth Order.

    Includes Index.

    1. Birth order.   2. Typology (Psychology)
    3. Personality.   I. Title
    BF698.3.I82   1988   155.9'24   87-35793
    ISBN 0-945156-00-6

Dedicated to my wife Kathy and our children: Duane, Mary, Shirley, Linda and Kevin.

— TABLE OF CONTENTS —

Introduction

What you understand, you can change. When you know your birth order, you can make changes in your behavior you never thought possible. You can adopt new, effective strategies for success in friendships, marriage and career. When you know others' birth orders, you can develop satisfying relationships while avoiding costly errors of judgment.

The birth order concepts in this book have helped thousands of people over the past seventeen years. Through birth order, they have been able to comprehend an otherwise confusing array of behaviors. They have found birth order to be a road map into the sometimes puzzling territory of human behavior.

My experience in using birth order began by counseling a man in marital conflict. He was in his thirties, father of two children. In a fit of anger, he had left his wife a few days before, shouting at her to get a divorce. By the time he came to me he was regretting his words to his wife, and hoping to undo the damage he had done.

With tears streaming down his face, he confessed his feelings of jealousy which were at the root of his anger. Although his wife had given him no reason to suspect infidelity, he would get angry if she so much as talked to another man, or took longer on an errand than he thought

1

she should. On the night he left, she had stopped to have coffee with friends before coming home from shopping.

It became apparent, as we talked, that his jealousy was related to his position in the family in which he grew up. Since he had been the youngest of seven brothers, the older boys could and did take away his toys at will. Later, when he was a teenager, they took away his girl friends. It was understandable that for him the world was full of older brothers who could take away his wife whenever they wanted. By his jealousy he attempted to keep his wife out of their reach. He could not control the world so he tried to control her.

With help, he was able to identify the fears he brought from his childhood experience. He was able to see that he was out of touch with the reality in which he was living as an adult. He developed new feelings of being loved by realizing his wife had chosen him rather than someone else. He realized she was a person with her own mind, rather than a toy to be snatched away by someone else. With this new understanding, he was able to stop trying to keep his wife out of the reach of other men. He was able to give up his jealousy without the inner struggle he would have experienced without the new insight.

In the thousands of counseling sessions since, I have always asked for birth order information. Much of what I share with you in this book is what I learned from my counselees.

Understanding birth order will not necessarily enable you to manipulate other persons, or accurately predict human behavior, or dominate others. Birth order knowledge may help you to understand human behavior, feel good about fellow human beings and handle yourself well. Birth order knowledge may also help you avoid manipulation by others who would take advantage of your birth order limitations.

Understanding the birth order concept may help you overcome communication barriers which are rooted in birth order characteristics.

Understanding birth order can enable parents to understand their children's thinking, feeling and behavior. Parents who understand their children may find themselves feeling confident, rather than frustrated, in their parenting. Children who feel understood by their parents will often relate with more geniality toward them.

Understanding birth order can help marital relationships. Spouses who understand each other's birth order, and their own, can resolve differences between them more easily. Your spouse may appear more sensible, when you understand how birth order affects him/her.

Understanding the effects of birth order can enable an employer to assign employees according to their strengths. An employer who knows birth order is more likely to discern which employee is apt to be the best salesman, bookkeeper or manager. An employer will probably get better service from employees who are satisfied because they are doing work which fits their birth order.

Understanding birth order effects can help immensely in counseling. The counselor who understands birth order effects will probably be able to identify problem areas, causes and useful interventions more quickly. Counseling can be brief, effective and satisfying for the counselor and counselee.

This book is written to give you an understanding of birth order from its development in childhood to its effects in adult life. Since human beings are complex, creative creatures, everything may not exactly fit the people you know. Perhaps, what you learn will not fit you precisely. However, what you learn can help you to a happier, more satisfying life.

How Birth Order Effects Develop

Most people who have come for counseling at our center have developed characteristics of first, second, third, fourth or only child birth order positions. Strong birth order characteristics may increase the need for counseling.

COPING STRATEGIES

Birth order effects, which are behaviors peculiar to each birth order position, develop as coping strategies a child uses to feel okay in his/her particular position in the family. These coping strategies can be to please, to be perfect, to be strong, to try hard, or to hurry. The extent to which this child needs these strategies to survive emotionally within the family probably determines this child's commitment to the birth order strategies throughout life. The more committed this child is to birth order strategies, the more likely he/she is to keep using them even if they cause problems rather than work to accomplish their purposes.

Children develop birth order strategies for coping with siblings rather than in response to parents. Except for the first born and the only child, children develop birth order characteristics by coping with the next older child. The second born must cope with the over-achieving first born, the third born must cope with a perfectionistic second born, and the fourth born must cope with a strong-willed third born. The first born must cope with loss of attention to the second born and the only with having to play alone. Out of these relationships each develops his/her own birth order characteristics.

FIRST BORN AS AN ONLY

Chronological order does not always determine a child's birth order position. For example, the first born can remain an only child psychologically if someone helps care for this child until he/she gets used to the baby. It may take only two weeks to a month of special care from a grandmother or other relative for the first born to remain an only child psychologically. If the first born remains an only child, the second child will usually take on the first born characteristics (or the only child characteristics if there are no more children). These exceptions commonly occur when there is little age difference between the first and second child since mother would be more likely to require help with the oldest child.

When the first born is an only child psychologically, there will often be conflict between the first and second child. In this case, the first born will usually resent the intrusions of the second child into his/her activity. A true first born would welcome the intrusion as an opportunity to demonstrate superiority over the second born.

The birth order tends to start over when there exists a large age difference of five or more years between siblings.

PARENT AS SIBLING

A parent, acting as a sibling, can divert the psychological birth order position of a child from the chronological position. A parent can do this, either by acting as a buddy to the child, or by engaging in severe conflict with the child. This usually happens between a mother and a daughter rather than a father and son because mother and daughter are likely to have more time together. It rarely happens between parent and child of opposite sex.

If a mother is second born, for instance, her daughter may become a third born in personality characteristics regardless of her position in the family. The daughter will take the position which follows the mother's birth order when mother acts like a sister rather than a parent. This may happen with any parent except the only child parent. Since there is no birth order that follows the only child, this parent would probably fail to influence the birth order of his/her child. In the case of a fourth born parent, the child affected by the parent can become a first born psychologically.

A child who is especially close to the parent of the opposite sex, may adopt the parent's birth order. The parental effect on birth order becomes even stronger if the other parent is of the next older birth order. For example, regardless of family placement, a son can become second born psychologically if he is emotionally close to a second born mother and in conflict with a first born father.

REMEMBERED CHILDREN

Sometimes, a child who is stillborn or dies in infancy is included in the family order. If this child continues to live on in the imagination of family members, the next younger sibling may adopt the next birth order position as if this child were actually present.

7

MULTIPLE BIRTHS

Twins and triplets apparently organize themselves into appropriate birth order positions. For example, twins who follow a first born may adopt positions in which one is second and the other third born rather than both becoming second born. Occasionally, twins appear to alternate birth orders with each other. The child who follows the twins will usually be of the next birth order, following the last birth order of the twins.

LARGE FAMILIES

Birth order in large families starts over with the fifth, ninth, thirteenth, and seventeenth child. Since the fourth born usually ignores the next child during the formative years, the cycle starts over with the child who follows the fourth born. The fifth child becomes a first born, the sixth a second born, and so on.

SET BY AGE FIVE

Birth order characteristics appear to be set by age five. In some instances, birth order characteristics appear to be set by age two or three. In one instance, a second born girl remained an only child psychologically into adulthood because her grandparents took care of her for two years before she became part of her family. Once birth order characteristics are set, children tend to modify rather than switch birth order characteristics when situations are changed.

First Born

The first born child is an only child until the second child is born. While the first born is an only child, he/she will get attention from parents, grandparents and others without having to compete for it.

Parents know the situation will be changed for the oldest child with the coming of the second child, so they often try to prepare the first born for the new baby. They encourage the first born to feel the kicks of the new baby in mommy's abdomen. They solicit his/her opinions of the nursery. They inform him/her what a baby requires, how much fun a baby is, and how small the baby will be. In anticipation, the first born may become quite excited about the coming of this new baby. Parents may actually increase the amount and quality of attention they give to the first born because they know that when the baby arrives, this child will have to share mother's attention. However, the first born child may not realize what sharing attention means until after the new baby arrives.

The new baby is not nearly as much fun as the first born anticipated. Instead of being fun, the new baby makes the first born uncomfortable by taking away mother's attention. Baby comes first with mother, and often with others as well.

Never before did the first born get put off when wanting

attention. Now, this child has to wait for the baby to be fed and go to sleep before he/she can sit in the lap that was so available before this "intruder" came. The first born has to bide his/her time for baby's needs to be met before his/her needs are met.

A few minutes can seem like hours to the two or three-year-old child who is waiting while mother takes care of the baby. Because time seems long, the first born may come to believe that mother loves baby more. Feeling unloved, this child may decide he/she has to earn love to be loved. Consequently, love appears to be conditioned on his/her behavior, rather than unconditional. With this perception, the only child becomes, psychologically, a first born. Moreover, from this moment, this child will tend to believe love is only available on a limited basis. Even when available, the first born believes he/she has to earn it.

The first born will often experiment with different ways of getting attention. By trying out different behaviors, this child usually discovers that anger, tantrums and whining do not get the desired attention. However, doing something to win approval often works better than anything else. Earning approval feels good and suggests useful activities for those long periods of waiting for mother to get through with the baby. So, when the opportunity presents itself, the first born brings mother a wash cloth to bathe the baby, plays patiently while keeping an eye on mother until she lays the baby down, and generally behaves like a "big" boy or girl. Mother's approving words, looks, and touches, confirm for the first born that he/she is earning love.

Love that is earned takes the form of approval, admiration and respect. To get this conditional attention which passes for love, the first born seeks approval from superiors, admiration from equals and respect from inferiors. In seeking this attention, the first born usually gives up asking for what he/she wants. In order to ask, the first born would have to assume he/she is worthy of being loved. Rather than asking, the first born hopes to receive what he/she wants by pleasing others.

To get approval, the first born often feels compelled to please almost everyone. The first born often compromises his/her own desires, needs and wants in order to win the approval of others to the point of forgetting what he/she wants. He/she can feel burdened, put upon and unfulfilled, while catering to others for their approval.

Others may dislike the first born's approval-seeking ways because they find the first born to be wishy-washy, indecisive and unassertive. They may get tired of always having to give approval, wishing the first born would express what he/she wants instead. In seeking approval, the first born may lose the very love he/she wants.

A first born person can rediscover what it feels like to be loved by taking the risk of asking for what he/she wants. By asking others for information, suggestions, help, time, and attention, the first born can recapture the early feeling of having love available for the asking.

In a social gathering, a first born may feel out of place unless he/she is able to contribute. When a first born is unable to do something in the group to win approval, admiration or respect, he/she may feel alienated. By asking for attention from members of the group, a first born can experience unconditional love within that setting.

In his/her private thoughts, the first born may fantasize impressive accomplishments which will bring amazed admiration from friends, associates and acquaintances. When the first born does accomplish something, he/she will tend to "get high" on the admiration. However, since humility is admirable, the first born may also act humble while secretly enjoying the admiration.

In seeking admiration, the first born may become an over-achiever. This person may work long hours, try to achieve perfection, be highly disciplined, do creative thinking and expend great effort in trying to get admiration from others. The first born can also be laid back, lazy, obnoxious, delinquent, lawless, or violent, if these qualities impress the important people in his/her life.

The first born may show the worst side of his/her character by demanding respect of those whom he/she perceives to be in an inferior position. This may translate into demands for instant obedience from children, pets, appliances, employees or spouse. If this obedience is not forthcoming immediately, the first born may get angry for not being given due respect. The first born adult may smash the electric can opener when it does not work, abuse a pet or a child who does not obey or turn against a spouse who appears disrespectful. To have personal worth, the first born may feel the need to require respect, regardless of consequences. One consequence may be the loss of love from family members.

Though the first born chooses to please others rather than self, he/she may eventually feel resentment at ''having'' to do that. Yet, despite the resentment, a first born may never confront others for fear they will turn away. Always, the first born puts the desires of others first for fear of losing whatever attention they may give. Sometimes, it appears, the first born will do almost anything to keep from losing approval, admiration or respect. Life may become one big compromise for the first born.

Paradoxically, the first born tends to lose the very attention he/she craves. In seeking approval or admiration, a first born may convince others so effectively that he/she does not need attention that others fail to give it. In one instance, a first born woman who played piano for church was constantly overlooked when accolades were given. Choir directors, worship leaders, committee chairpersons, Sunday School teachers and ushers were recognized, but the piano player was overlooked. To gain their approval, she had convinced them that she played only for the joy of playing. Consequently, no one realized she would have liked a pat on the back, too.

The first born's tendency to compromise can frustrate those who must deal with this person. The first born may compromise by making conflicting commitments beyond his/her ability to fulfill them. Though others may disapprove of the first born's failure to keep promises, the first born is not apt to refuse requests by saying, "I have already promised to do something else so I cannot do what you ask." The first born will try to accommodate everyone in order to get maximum approval, admiration and respect.

Since first borns usually seek respect from family and approval from others, they will be more demanding of family members than of others. If family members complain, the first born will tend to get angry, rather than change his/her behavior.

After an encounter with others outside family, first borns tend to castigate themselves for not doing enough to get approval or admiration. For example, after a conversation, a first born may examine it mentally, feeling guilty if he/she might have said anything which could have offended the other person.

The first born adult may often fear making someone else into a victim. Remembering the pain of rejection as a child, the first born tries to behave in such a way that no one will be made to feel rejected. However, since adults are not as vulnerable as children, a first born may inappropriately try to take care of others' feelings for them.

The first born will often feel tears when someone receives special recognition. The first born is especially touched if the person being honored has been overlooked for a period of time before being discovered as a worthy object of honor. For example, a first born may shed tears while watching a TV show in which a child who has done

13

well is finally honored after being overlooked.

Caring touches a first born more than admiration. When told, "I care about you," the first born is more likely to shed tears than when told, "I admire you." The tears testify to the emotional sacrifice the first born made to adjust to the presence of his/her siblings as a small child.

In order to satisfy their desires for conditional love, first borns tend to go into helping professions. They want to help people whom, they anticipate, will give them the approval, admiration and respect they crave. They often aspire to leadership for the same reason.

To overcome the limits of birth order position, the first born needs to value his/her desires, wants and needs as much as those of others. The first born needs to discover that when others know what he/she wants, they may not only respect those wants, but appreciate knowing what they are. It may help the first born to realize that taking care of everyone else's wants is not necessary for him/her to be happy, have good relationships, or get what he/she wants.

A first born may fear becoming insensitive to others' feelings when he/she cares for self. This would happen only if a first born tries to overcome birth order characteristics by repressing the desires for approval, admiration and respect. He/she may then try to "prove" that these kinds of attention are not important by becoming obnoxious. For the first born to remain sensitive to people, it is better to solicit unconditional love rather than suppress the desire for earned love (conditional love). Feeling loved can render the pursuit of approval, admiration and respect unnecessary.

Second Born

The second born child has to cope early in life with the first born's attempts to impress parents at his/her expense. When the second born accomplishes something, the first born seizes the opportunity to obtain approval by out-performing him/her. By choosing the right time to show off, the first born can arrange for an audience who will give positive strokes. The second born can easily feel inadequate because he/she cannot do as well.

The second born cannot cope with the first born's behavior by reasoning that competence will come with age. Rather than feeling reassured by noting the age difference, this child may decide, "I cannot do anything well." Throughout life, the second born may struggle, trying to overcome the feeling of inadequacy created by this decision.

The second born usually chooses a strategy of perfectionism to overcome the feeling of inadequacy. This child believes that doing something perfectly could create a feeling of okayness. However, realizing that not everything can be done perfectly, this child usually selects a restricted arena in which to attempt perfection.

In this chosen field of endeavor, the second born tries to get every detail right. For example, a second born child, who makes a small mistake in a drawing, may start the drawing over rather than let it exist with the flaw. This child may do a page of homework over rather than have an erasure. For the second born, every detail must be right in the chosen realm of perfection.

The perfectionism of the second born is often overlooked because it does not extend to every area of life. The second born child may have a messy room, may not care about what he/she eats, and may ignore personal appearance while being meticulous about preparing a piano recital to perfection.

Even though performing well, the second born fails to overcome the feeling of inadequacy through perfect-ionism. The feeling of inadequacy can continue to influence the thinking, feeling and behavior of the second born for a lifetime.

A second born may fantasize perfect performance to overcome the feeling of inadequacy. These fantasies may help the second born perform more adequately or may become a substitute for actual performance.

The second born adult may try to overcome feelings of inadequacy by making other persons feel less adequate. Second borns may withhold compliments which would allow others to take pride in their own performance, and give criticism, correction and suggestions which highlight the inadequacy of others' achievements. If others react to the negative feedback, the second born may modify the strategy by giving carefully selected compliments and offering suggestions more kindly, but without actually relinquishing the attempt to reduce the imaginary adequacy gap. The second born simply becomes more subtle. To give positive, encouraging compliments and to stop criticizing, the second born must be able to feel adequate.

The second born may try to overcome the feeling of inadequacy by limiting the opportunities for performance on the part of spouse, children, employees, associates and others. As an adult, the second born may curtail what others do by requiring that certain conditions be met before they may do what they want to do. For example, in an organization, the second born may require that policies, which may not be necessary, be written before programs for action can be pursued. The subconscious purpose of these restrictions is to make the second born feel less inadequate by making others feel more inadequate.

By this strategy, the second born in power tends to destroy motivation in people by restraining their initiative, rejecting their ideas and hindering them from exercising power. For example, the second born who assigns a task may also prescribe, in detail, how the task is to be done. By so doing, the second born relegates the other person to the position of servant rather than allowing the person to think, decide and act independently to accomplish the task.

As a child, the second born may have longed to dethrone the first born who was causing the feelings of inadequacy. This longing may become a subconscious drive which continues to make a second born hope to humble first borns. Though the second born may succeed in dethroning a first born, the feeling of inadequacy will persist. The feeling comes from within, not from the behavior of other people.

In courting perfection, a second born tends to prefer logic over feelings. For example, a second born husband may respond to his wife's expression of unhappiness by giving her several logical reasons why she should be happy. Rather than cheering up his wife, this reasoning probably depresses her even more by suggesting that her feelings are wrong. She would be comforted better by his caring for her, rather than by his doing her thinking for her. However, though he may care deeply, he may feel too inadequate to comfort his wife emotionally. He would prefer to express his caring by giving advice or by analyzing. Remaining logical allows him to feel more adequate.

A second born may threaten his/her marital relationship by remaining logical when the spouse needs emotional contact. In one instance, a second born man was puzzled when his wife left him after he had tried to be a model husband. He provided well, helped her with household chores and was faithful. Since he did many good things, he could not understand why she would not accept his "constructive criticism" and "reasonable limitations." She never became reconciled to him, though friends and family encouraged her to do so because "he was such a good man." They could not comprehend, nor could he, how his use of logic ruined this relationship. Regardless of other considerations, she could no longer tolerate his reasoning as a response to her feelings. She might have stayed in the marriage if she could have come to believe he cared about how she felt.

In certain situations, the sense of inadequacy, with its accompanying perfectionism, is an asset. For instance, a second born man took a failing company and over several years built it into a profitable concern. He succeeded because he was trying to overcome his feeling of inadequacy by resurrecting this company. However, when the company became a success he experienced burnout, because his feelings of inadequacy returned. His feelings of inadequacy were diminished as long as he worked with a struggling business. His attention to detail, his ability to control and his perfectionism put the business on its feet. But the success he experienced did not wipe out the feelings of inadequacy, which had been kept at bay by his struggle to achieve.

Sometimes, a second born will avoid the feeling of inadequacy by going from job to job, quitting each time success is achieved, in order to start from the bottom of a new job. Some second borns stay in a lesser position to keep from getting into a challenging environment which could cause them to feel inadequate.

Because of their perfectionism, second borns tend to

like to work with finances. Not all second borns like mathematics, but those who do, often find themselves working in financial institutions where they not only are able to work with the perfection of numbers, but where they also have the opportunity to limit others.

To achieve perfection, the second born teenager may practice facial expressions, posture and movements in front of a mirror. Perfectionism may not be achieved, but the second born often is more expressive, has a better figure and moves more gracefully than persons of other birth orders. The second born, who has spent hours in front of the mirror, can be a very attractive person.

The second born can be refreshingly candid in giving feedback. Some of the negative feedback can be very useful to others. If you can evaluate the criticism of the second born apart from the apparent attempt to dethrone, you will often discover helpful information. Paying attention to the second borns in your life may help you avoid making costly mistakes.

Third Born

The third born child develops birth order strategies to defend against the second born's attempts to pass on the feeling of inadequacy.

Children often believe it is possible to get rid of bad feelings by passing them on to someone else when the opportunity presents itself. The second born sees such an opportunity with the third born. The third born will have to develop strategies which will counteract the second born's attempts to pass on inadequacy. These strategies to cope with the second born's behavior are usually developed by the third born within the first five years, and often within the first two or three years.

By experimenting, the second born usually discovers that ridicule seems to create feelings of inadequacy in the third born. Being able to make fun of the third born's efforts allows the second born to imagine that the third born feels more inadequate than he/she does. However, rather than feeling inadequate, the third born tends to feel vulnerable. Through ridicule, the second born seems to be able to make the third born uncomfortable, almost at will. The third born may feel defenseless against that assault.

At first, the third born may appeal to mother for relief from the second born's ridicule. Since mother is usually unable to keep the second born from getting to the third born, she may tell the third born to ignore the second born in order to stop the conflict between them. By so doing, she is suggesting the strategy most third borns adopt.

By ignoring the taunts, put-downs, and ridicule of the second born, the third born can feel strong. Turning off feelings seems more powerful than arguing, appealing to mom or getting angry in dealing with the second born. By experience, the third born discovers this strategy does counteract the second born's tactics.

Not only does the third born feel stronger by becoming impervious to the second born's attacks, he/she frustrates the second born with the "it doesn't bother me" attitude. Success encourages the third born to continue, expand and perfect this birth order strategy.

The third born can refine and develop his/her birth order strategy by becoming fearless. By becoming fearless, the third born is often able to do normally frightening things, shrug off negative criticism, and continue his/her behavior in the face of threatening consequences.

While able to eliminate much fear, the third born is unable to eliminate fear completely. In those instances where fear remains, the third born will usually avoid whatever causes the fear. The third born's greatest fear could be of fear itself.

The fearlessness of the third born child can make this child difficult for adults to control. Common adult attempts to control by punishment, threats and intimidation, may not work with the third born. The third born may actually do what is forbidden in order to "prove" that these adult ploys do not frighten him/her. Parents who try to intimidate the third born child may create more problems than they solve.

A disproportionate percentage of youth who get into trouble appear to be third borns. A social worker reported that at a girls' half-way house where she worked, 47 of the 54 girls in custody were third borns.

If a third born is pushed into doing something he/she fears, the third born may translate the fear into anger before doing the feared activity. A third born may be angry most of the time, if pushed into enough fearful activity. For example, a man who pushed his third born wife into a public speaking career, which she feared, later complained that she was constantly angry. She had adjusted by turning her fear into anger.

Third born children are the most likely to be bored. While other children can make life exciting by doing what is scary for them, third borns lose the stimulation by refusing to do scary things. Without this stimulation, third borns can become bored.

Third borns tend to have a strong sense of empathy for weak and helpless persons with whom they tend to identify. This empathy is often expressed by third borns through working in nursing homes, sheltered workshops and other helping institutions.

The sense of empathy with the spirit of fearlessness can give the third born an unusual ability to sell. In selling, the third born is often able to approach people fearlessly, relate to them with empathy and shrug off rejection in order to approach the next prospect. Many successful sales people are third borns.

Third borns often determine quickly whether they can feel safe with a stranger. Third borns will usually reject or avoid persons with whom they do not feel safe. When feeling threatened by someone, a third born can be as insulting and harsh as necessary to turn that person away.

By seeking non-threatening relationships, a third born child may choose friends who are unacceptable to parents. A third born child may be drawn to non-achieving children rather than achievers of whom the parents would approve. If parents should try to select their third born's friends, they may find themselves in severe conflict with their child. A third born child, when feeling vulnerable, may strongly resist having to associate with children whom the parents choose. If the child should decide to abide by his/her parents' wishes, he/she may experience painful inner conflict.

The third born can learn to use vulnerability itself as a defense. Rather than arguing, the third born may dismiss the second born with a "do whatever you think is right." This strategy derails the second born's attempt to pass on the feeling of inadequacy. In effect, the third born forces the second born to face the feeling of inadequacy by telling him/her to do what is right.

To keep from feeling vulnerable, a third born may want to maintain emotional distance from others. This can be done by using humor which can become tiresome with time. A spouse may become unhappy with the third born's "lack of seriousness." By using humor to move people away emotionally, the third born can irritate those who want to be close.

When the spouse of a third born expresses feelings, especially negative feelings, the third born may refuse to respond or respond by telling the spouse, "Don't let it bother you." Being confronted with feelings can make the third born feel uncomfortably vulnerable. For the third born to be open to another's feelings, the person expressing them must be non-threatening. A spouse may feel threatening since the third born cannot simply withdraw from this relationship.

A third born who is feeling vulnerable will tend to withdraw from family and friends. This person may have one friend with whom to share confidences, while maintaining distance from everyone else. Quite often, the third born chooses a friend, other than the spouse, in whom to confide, and if this person happens to be of the opposite sex, may become involved in an affair.

Paradoxically, third borns tend to take total responsibility for close relationships, rather than share responsiblity with the other person. Third borns usually do not confront, argue or disagree with persons who are important to them. Without shared responsibility, their relationships often do not develop the closeness they crave.

In order to have intimate, satisfying relationships, third borns may need to develop an emotional defense system which will allow them to interact with others without feeling vulnerable. Learning how to take care of themselves emotionally, third borns could risk confronting others in order to create closer, more satisfying ties with them.

Parents can help a third born child by giving him/her permission for self defense. In fact, parents may find this to be the most effective way to encourage their third born child to choose better friends. When the third born child is free to stand up for himself/herself in relationships, he/she can choose new friends more freely. In other words, permission to be assertive enables the third born to feel secure with more people.

Third borns sometimes look for an emotional defense system in religion, particularly religion which promises supernatural protection. When frightened, this person can use religion as a place of retreat to keep from feeling vulnerable. This defense system can be so important to the third born, that he/she will resist any suggestion to examine the basis of the faith he/she has espoused. Rather than analyze, the third born may want to simply trust the protection his/her faith promises.

While avoiding close relationships, a third born can be quite creative in providing alternatives to closeness. This person can offer ideas, strategies and insights which can enhance life for others, even though the subsconscious motivation may be to achieve security by maintaining distance from them. A third born can keep you busy looking at things so that you will not be looking at him/her.

Fourth Born

When a fourth born arrives in this world, he/she already has three older siblings. Of these siblings, the third born is going to have the greatest impact on the fourth.

The third born would like to become more comfortable by passing on the discomfort of vulnerability to someone else. Since the fourth born appears to be vulnerable already by being younger, the third born usually tries to pass the feeling to this child.

The third born takes the opportunity to pass on that feeling when the fourth born has matured enough to play with the other children. To make the fourth born to feel vulnerable, the third born tells this child that he/she is not old enough, big enough, fast enough, tall enough, capable enough, or experienced enough, to join the three older children in their play. Though the third born is trying to make the fourth born feel vulnerable, he/she tends to make the fourth born feel immature instead. If mother intervenes by insisting that the older children include the fourth born in their activities, the fourth born can feel even more immature as the three older ones protest, "Aw Mom, he/she will just slow us down." Therefore, having often been reminded of his/her immaturity, the fourth born may decide, "I will never be grown up." Having learned to perceive self as immature, the fourth born may feel immature for a lifetime.

The fourth born person, who has decided he/she will never be grown up, may appear to be unable to grow up. This person may have trouble being serious. He/she may fail to take on responsibility when requested by someone else (though he or she may do prodigious feats on his/her own initiative). When challenged, he/she may withdraw into an emotional shell. The fourth born may even prefer playing with children to keeping company with adults. Others are often tempted to tell the fourth person to grow up.

When challenged, the fourth born may insist he/she does not want to grow up. While others may accept aging as inevitable, the fourth born may seem determined to stay young. In fact, the fourth born may not be able to imagine getting old.

Even though the fourth born feels immature, he/she may want to be mature. To learn how to grow up, the fourth born often observes that others demonstrate their maturity by doing difficult things. When the third born convinces the fourth born that he/she cannot do what they can, the fourth born comes to believe that growing up means doing difficult things. It appears logical to the fourth born that, by trying hard enough, he/she can be grown up.

Occasionally, the fourth born succeeds in keeping up with the older children by sheer effort. This success reinforces the strategy of trying hard as a way of overcoming the feeling of immaturity. As an adult, the fourth born may endure difficulties that could be resolved. This person may reject effective ways of doing things because they appear too easy. Doing things the hard way allows the fourth born to feel mature, or so he/she thinks.

Fourth borns, attempting to feel grown up, can tolerate much suffering. For example, a fourth born may put up with a difficult relationship, a difficult job or a difficult situation rather than accept a reasonable alternative. The fourth born may believe that to escape difficulty is to let the world know how immature he/she really is. Therefore, the fourth born may feel compelled to reject a more comfortable option, even though it could be a rational alternative to a difficult life situation.

The fourth born may have trouble understanding that a person can be mature and do things the easy way at the same time. This person does not realize that as a person matures, it becomes easier to do tasks which once were difficult. Thus, doing things the easy way, which the fourth born rejects, is actually an indication of maturity.

The fourth born may dislike being asked to do something, since any task may appear to be difficult work. This person may not believe you when you suggest a task is easy, thinking, "It might be easy for you, but it is difficult for me." On the other hand, a fourth born may be offended when asked to do something easy, as if the request were a suggestion that he/she is too immature to do difficult things.

Fourth borns sometimes feel used when they are asked to do something. The feeling comes from childhood, when they were used by the older children to do things for them. Though they served the older children, they were not accepted as equals by them. As adults, fourth borns will tend to feel used when others make requests of them, unless they feel they are being accepted by them.

The feeling of being excluded sometimes leads a young fourth born woman to marry a man a several years older than herself, hoping that he will include her in the society of which he is a part. Since the husband probably chose her for her immaturity, he is usually more interested in keeping her the way she was than in getting her accepted by others. Consequently, he may try to keep her immature by restricting her opportunities for growth through social contacts, work experiences and education. He may keep trying to limit her growth until she becomes unwilling to accept the boundaries he places on her. This marriage is often in jeopardy when she gets into her late twenties or early thirties.

Problems can occur when fourth borns feel more at home with children than adults. Many men who commit incest are fourth born children who, as adults, emotionally and sexually relate better to children than to adults. They may feel neither shame nor guilt for having committed incest since, perceiving themselves as children, they hold their children just as much or more responsible for the incest as themselves.

As a child, being immature meant the fourth born had trouble getting others to listen. There were three older siblings and a set of parents with whom he/she had to compete for a chance to be heard. Perhaps the child had to get someone to listen by pounding on that person's thigh with little fists. The feeling that no one will listen can cause the fourth born adult to attempt to force others to hear by talking loudly or by hitting. Having hit a spouse or a child, the fourth born may expect that person to relate as if it had not happened.

Feeling immature, the fourth born parent may try to change places with the first born child. In order to relieve the burden of being a parent, the fourth born may try to force the first born child to adopt a parental role with the other siblings. The fourth born parent may also try to make the child parent him/her by becoming dependent on the child. This parent may expect the young child to listen, understand and comfort him/her. Fourth born parents can force their children, especially their first born, to grow up too fast. This first born may experience childhood as responsibility rather than fun.

Having grown up under the power of older siblings, fourth borns may want to exercise power by getting into management type careers. Having achieved a position of power, their attitude of immaturity may cause them to adopt a "hands off" management style, which forces subordinates to solve problems their own way. Since subordinates soon learn to solve problems on their own, fourth born managers may view themselves as presiding over a big happy unit, blissfully unaware of the turmoil within the organization.

On the other hand, fourth borns can also supervise oppressively. This often happens in the home where a fourth born parent tries to control the behavior of spouse and children in detail. This parent will always be looking over the shoulder of family members to be sure they are doing things right.

To keep others from getting to them, fourth borns tend to stop listening when someone says something they do not want to hear. Having withdrawn, they can feel secure while the other person beats on their psychological shell. If someone penetrates the shell by getting through with an unwelcome message, fourth borns can suffer excruciating emotional pain. They may get extremely upset, desperately seek reassurance, or strike out at others.

In a family of more than four children, the fourth born usually tries to pass on the feeling of being left out by ignoring the fifth born. This has the effect of starting the birth order over again with the fifth child.

Only Child

The only child develops birth order characteristics while trying to avoid excessive attention from the parents and while playing alone without the company of siblings.

Other children may envy the only child who does not have to compete for the attention of parents. However, when the attention becomes oppressive, the only child may wish his/her parents had other children to whom they could pay attention. Sometimes, the only child would like to be left alone.

To understand how excessive attention affects the child, imagine how the child feels as parents enter his/her play. Rather than feeling grateful, the child may feel disappointed when the parents try to show him/her how to have more fun by playing differently. Instead of appreciating the attention, this child may resent the interference which takes away the joy of discovery through experimentation. Being told how to play takes some of the fun out of playing.

To deal with parental intrusion, the only child may develop fast and slow speeds for doing things. This child develops a fast speed in order to finish projects before others can interfere with them. For example, an only child may color a picture very quickly to keep parents from trying to help with it. As an adult, the only child may still do enjoyable tasks quickly, as if doing the tasks more slowly may allow others to mar the joy by interfering.

On the other hand, the only child develops a slow speed for giving others the opportunity to help get the task done. For example, when the time comes to put toys back in the toy box, the only child goes into slow motion, knowing that someone will help put them away. Similarly, as an adult, the only child may still work slowly when doing unpleasant tasks. However, the adult only child may become frustrated with himself/herself for procrastinating with unpleasant tasks rather than actually getting help in doing them.

Unfortunately, doing pleasant tasks quickly and unpleasant tasks slowly minimizes pleasure and maximizes work for the only child. Consequently, life may seem to be a lot of work without much fun.

Furthermore, the only child is often unable to separate work from play. When the only child adult is working, especially at home, he/she may "steal" time to play. Work will be put off to watch a little TV, have a snack or read the sports page. On the other hand, when the only child does do something for fun, he/she will tend to worry about what "needs to be done" rather than fully enjoying the fun.

The only child probably began to have difficulty separating work from play when parents insisted the child do something he/she did not feel like doing. Therefore, having stopped play reluctantly, this child may continue thinking about having fun while doing what the parents want. If this child protests against doing something, the parents may inform him/her that some things "have to be done." Consequently, this child may learn to worry about those things that "have to be done" while playing. As an adult, this person may be unable to work without thinking about play, or play without thinking about work.

As the only child gets older, parents tend to guide their

child more than is necessary, rather than permit their child to reason for himself/herself. As a result, to escape unwanted advice, the only child may try to do things so well that no advice need be given. Consequently, the only child may appear to be perfectionistic. However, the only child does not usually focus on details, as does the second born, but on the larger picture.

Furthermore, having become sensitive to intrusive advice, the only child may also resent criticism. In fact, once criticized for something, the only child may try to avoid doing the behavior which was criticized, even if the criticism was unwarranted.

The only child often feels smothered at home by too much attention. However, going to school enables the only child to escape attention. At school, the only child discovers a world in which normal attention makes relationships free and easy. Being at school, this child feels liberated from the stifling effect of someone watching over his/her shoulder. It feels good to get away from home.

As a result, the only child may become conditioned to feeling stifled at home and feeling free away from home. Even as an adult, this person may feel oppressed at home but liberated when working at a job, having lunch in a restaurant, or visiting in someone else's home. An understanding husband or wife can create greater rapport with an only child spouse by finding opportunities to be together outside the home.

It is not impossible for an only child to enjoy time at home. He/she can enjoy time at home if he/she is alone or if other family members are too occupied to intrude. Special times which are planned ahead, such as parties, can also be enjoyed by the only child.

In order to cope with having to play alone, the only child often creates an imaginary sibling for companionship. This sibling could be completely imaginary, or be embodied in a doll, teddy bear or pet. Since this companion does not have feelings or personality, the only child provides these qualities. In other words, the only child furnishes both sides of the relationship. Therefore, the only child has to consider only his/her own feelings, thoughts and attitudes while playing with the imaginary sibling. In creating this relationship the only child discovers a way to feel comfortable alone, a way which can work for a lifetime.

Consequently, having learned to relate to imaginary companions, the only child will tend to ignore the feelings, attitudes and thoughts of others. Turned inward, the only child may respond to another's feelings by talking about his/her own feelings. Unfortunately, because the only child tends to listen to self rather than others, he/she may appear to be self-centered. For this reason, some people perceive only children as "spoiled."

Nevertheless, only children are not usually "spoiled" in the sense of demanding many things. Their attention may be turned inward to their own attitudes, feelings and goals rather than outwardly to others, but they are not necessarily "spoiled." "Spoiled" children are those who identify love with the things others can give them. Unlike "spoiled" children, only children commonly learned to feel loved by being loved, rather than by receiving things as substitutes for love.

However, only children do value personal things, which they may regard subconsciously as friends. For example, an only child may name his/her car, talk about it as though it had feelings, and care for it lovingly. Familiar objects are friends who make the only child person feel comfortable alone. Accordingly, if the only child were to lose everything familiar in a fire or other disaster, he/she could grieve for a long time. New things cannot take the place of the old, familiar things which provide emotional companionship.

The only child often learns to expect order in his/her world, since there are no siblings to disrupt order during the child's formative years. Accordingly, the only child, having gotten things organized, may expect things to stay that way. For example, when the only child adult has decided on a schedule of activities, he/she expects to follow it to the letter. If something interrupts that schedule, this person may feel that the whole day has been "ruined". Obviously, it appears "ruined" only because the only child feels compelled to reconstruct the whole schedule if part of it has been disrupted.

To understand this feeling, picture a table full of objects. Imagine that, though there is no more room on the table, something else has to be put on it. Faced with this problem, a person of another birth order will usually take something less important off the table to accommodate the new item. On the other hand, the only child may feel it necessary to clear off the table completely in order to fill it up again with the new item included. It may appear that the only child has trouble setting priorities.

In communicating with others, the only child tends to respond to logic with feelings and to feelings with logic. These responses were learned in childhood, when parental logic and emotions feel oppressive. Responding to parental logic with feelings and to parental feelings with logic gave the only child a useful form of defense. Consequently, as an adult, the only child can still use this defense to frustrate a spouse or others who try to get through to him/her. The only may talk about how he/she feels rather than thinking about the conversation.

If the spouse shares his/her feelings, especially unpleasant feelings, the only child partner may give advice rather than showing empathy. In fact, the only child tends to react rather than interact. As one only child adult put it, "I think with my feelings."

37

Identifying Yourself

As you have been reading, you have probably been trying to identify your own birth order position. No doubt you are puzzled if you found you possess characteristics of more than one birth order position. This chapter may help you to identify your own psychological birth order more precisely.

Your birth order effects may be mild if you grew up in a stable, secure and loving home. In such a home, you would have had less need to develop strong coping strategies. On the other hand, if you had to cope with a difficult home life as a child, you would be more likely to develop distinct birth order characteristics. Accordingly, the ease with which you can identify your own birth order may depend on your childhood experience.

If you were transferred from one birth order position to another in early childhood, you may have developed a modified set of birth order characteristics. As a result, your basic birth order position may not be clear. For example, a first born child could possess some second born characteristics, if placed into the second born position in a combined family.

However, your chronological placement in the family is the best place to begin analyzing your own birth order. More often than not, a person's psychological birth order position will be the same as his/her chronological position.

When psychological birth order position does not correspond to chronological birth order, there can be several explanations. For example, a first born child may continue to be an only child if someone, in addition to mother, took care of this child until he/she became accustomed to the new baby. If the first born should remain an only child psychologically, the second born child will usually be an only or a first born rather than a second born.

If you are one of several children, you may be able to identify your birth order in the family by finding the perfectionist among your siblings. Since this child will be a second born psychologically, you can count up or down from this child to yourself to find your birth order. If you are the perfectionist, you are the second born.

Age difference of five or more years can start the birth order over, but not always. Even with five years' age difference, you may need to analyze further to determine your birth order.

A child who dies at birth or in infancy may affect the birth order of children who follow, if the family feels the presence of this child as though he/she were still alive. Having to adjust to this presence forces the sibling who follows to adopt the appropriate birth order position.

Obviously, a child can hold any psychological birth order position, regardless of chronological position in the family. Accordingly, a birth order position may have to be determined on the basis of personality characteristics rather than placement in the family.

BEYOND CHRONOLOGY

If in doubt, you can confirm your birth order position by trying on the birth order T-shirts. Each T-shirt succinctly defines a birth order position by the sayings printed on it. As you consider the T-shirts, you may find one which expresses your feelings or attitudes. The shirt you choose may reveal your psychological birth order.

Before you read the explanations, try on the T-shirts, or let someone else suggest which one fits you. If one fits well, you have probably found your birth order.

The saying on the front expresses the birth order attitude toward life. The saying on the back reveals the thought behind the attitude on the front. Together, they summarize each birth order position.

The birth order T-shirt sayings are arranged in random order to enable you to consider all of them before making your decision.

FRONT: Life isn't easy.
BACK: You have to try hard.

FRONT: Leave me alone.
BACK: I'd rather do it myself.

FRONT: That won't work.
BACK: It's not good enough.

FRONT: I don't know.
BACK: What do you think?

FRONT: No problem.
BACK: It doesn't bother me any.

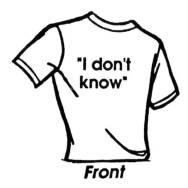

Front

THE FIRST BORN

The first born T-shirt says "I don't know", on the front and "What do you think?" on the back. The first born, having chosen approval, admiration and respect over unconditonal love, loses track of what he/she feels, wants or thinks. This person feels the need to know where others stand before becoming aware of his/her own position. The first born may literally say, "I don't know. What do you think?"

A first born tries to become oriented to the needs, feelings and attitudes of other people. This T-shirt invites others to tell their thoughts, so the first born knows what to think.

Back

Front

Back

THE SECOND BORN

The second born T-shirt says "That won't work" on the front and "It's not good enough" on the back. To overcome the feeling of inadequacy, the second born child tries, by finding fault, to keep the first born from out-performing him/her. Suppose, for example, a first born sibling decided to impress their parents by doing the dishes. The second born might undercut this effort by telling the parents how much soap the first born used or by pointing out the spots on the glasses.

By saying "that won't work", the second born puts others on the defensive. By focusing on details, the second born "proves" something will not work because "it is not good enough." This T-shirt portrays how a second born humbles the arrogant-appearing first born.

Front

THE THIRD BORN

The third born T-shirt says "no problem" on the front and "It doesn't bother me any" on the back. When the second born tried to convince the third born that something could not be done, the third born just said, "No problem," and did it anyway. To the second born's criticism, the third born replied, "It doesn't bother me any."

A third born, by not reacting, tries to become impervious to put-down strategies. This T-shirt demonstrates how a third born does it.

Back

Front

Back

THE FOURTH BORN

The fourth born T-shirt says "Life isn't easy" on the front and "You have to try hard" on the back. These sayings express the fourth born's frustration at being rejected on the basis of immaturity, by the third born. Life was not easy for this child when it came to playing with the older children. Since life was not easy for this child, he/she decided that, in order to cope, "You have to try hard."

The fourth born may try hard to be part of the world from which he/she feels excluded. This T-shirt portrays the fourth born's attitude toward life as he/she perceives it.

Front

THE ONLY CHILD

The only child T-shirt says "Leave me alone" on the front and "I'd rather do it myself" on the back. These sayings represent the only child's reaction to excessive attention by parents. As a result, even as an adult, the only child may want to keep others from intruding on his/her life. This person wishes to be left alone to do things in his/her own way.

Back

An only child wants to achieve his/her own accomplishments. This T-shirt asks the world to let him/her do it.

If none of these T-shirts seems to fit you, consider which one would have fit you when you were younger. Certain life experiences can blur birth order by causing you to adjust stategies and attitudes from what would be normal for you according to your birth order. Of course, behavior contrary to birth order may indicate you have been able to transcend some of the limitations of your birth order.

Another way to uncover psychological birth order is to determine who makes you uncomfortable. In terms of chronological birth order, the younger one discomforts the older one. A second born may make a first born uncomfortable, a third born may make the second born uncomfortable, and so on. The first born may make the fourth born uncomfortable since the fifth born, who is also a first born psychologically, follows the fourth born.

If you know that persons of a certain birth order make you uncomfortable, consider the possibility that you may be psychologically of the next older birth order.

If you still have trouble ascertaining your psychological birth order, observe the kind of difficulty you experience. A first born may have difficulty because he/she does not have insight. A second born may have difficulty because he/she cannot make all the details fit just right. A third born may have difficulty because the identification may make him/her feel vulnerable. A fourth born may make hard work out of understanding birth order. An only child may resist the analysis because it feels like an intrusion which he/she feels no one has a right to make. The kind of difficulty you have may, itself, be an indication of your psychological birth order.

Traits Vs. Strategies

You may hope that learning birth order characteristics may enable you to quickly identify the birth orders of new people you meet. Consequently, you may anticipate having an advantage over others in personal relationships. However, you will probably discover that it is often difficult to determine another person's birth order from casual conversation. Sometimes, you will find birth order to be obvious, but you may often be hard put to identify birth order from your first encounter. To recognize your birth order, you may need to know the person's background, behavior in various situations and attitudes toward life.

Birth order identification can be difficult because people can use birth order strategies other than their own. However, they will use them to accomplish their own goals. For example, a person of any birth order may employ perfectionism. A first born may use it to gain approval, a second born to feel adequate, a third born to feel safe, a fourth born to feel grown up, and an only child to try to do things right.

Persons in each of the birth orders can use the strategies of

impressing others
doing perfectly

pleasing others
trying hard
hurrying

to accomplish their own goals. The strategy a person uses may mislead you into thinking this person belongs to a particular birth order.

However, a person using a strategy foreign to his/her birth order position will relinquish it when it stops working. For example, a first born will drop perfectionism when it fails to impress others. A third born will drop it when it fails to overcome the feeling of vulnerability. A fourth born will drop it when it fails to make him/her feel more mature. An only child will drop it when it fails to help him/her do things right. Only a second born will tend to stay committed to perfectionism when it fails to accomplish his/her purposes.

Although a person may conceal birth order traits behind a variety of strategies in casual relationships, within the intimacy of a family a person will tend to use the strategies indigenous to his/her birth order. Therefore, to discover a person's birth order, observe how that person relates within the family. A person can seldom hide birth order characteristics while participating in intimate relationships.

Furthermore, stress can expose a person's birth order position since a person under stress will tend to revert to original birth order strategies. For example, a first born in a comfortable situation may pay attention to his/her own wants, needs and desires. But, when feeling pressured, the first born will usually return to seeking approval, admiration and respect. Unless a person overcomes birth order limitations, he/she will revert to them when under duress. Therefore, you can discover another's birth order position by observing how that person acts in stress-inducing situations.

Birth Order in Marriage

Many factors other than birth order affect a marriage. Differences in age, cultural background, education, and values can affect it. A couple's health, financial condition, number of children, relationship with in-laws, and intellectual compatibility can determine the level of harmony they experience. The nature and quality of support from others may determine how the marriage will fare in difficult times.

Therefore, your marriage may not fit the particular description of relationship according to birth order. However, you may gain valuable insight into your particular marriage even if all the details do not agree with your experience.

It is important to realize that birth order affects a marriage most powerfully when one or both partners come from traumatic backgrounds. In unhappy homes, birth order strategies become stronger as children learn to cope. These strong strategies, which are usually practiced rigidly, can create problems in a marriage.

Couples who come from happy homes have the best prospect for a happy marriage. Their marriage may escape the effects of birth order since they can be more flexible in relating to each other.

CHAPTER ORGANIZATION

This chapter is organized into five sections, corresponding to each birth order. In each section, the relationship of one birth order with each of the five birth orders is examined. Therefore, you can easily find the section that applies to you and within that section, find your particular birth order pairing.

FIRST BORN MARRIAGES

First borns tend to demand respect from their marriage partners. In demanding respect, a first born may try to humiliate the spouse to get it, thereby decreasing the chances for genuine love. While demanding respect from the spouse, a first born may be more considerate of others from whom he/she hopes to gain admiration or approval. Sometimes, a first born who is berating his/her spouse in an attempt to force respect, can change behavior dramatically for the better when a visitor stops in. This disparity of treatment between strangers and family can make the spouse resent the first born.

Two first borns, married to each other, tend to work harder at getting attention from others than in relating to each other. When courting, they exchange approval, respect and admiration with each other, but after the wedding they have trouble finding ways to love each other. In fact, they feel awkward just talking to each other. Unable to have a natural, loving relationship with each other, they may become mechanical with each other by doing what they are "supposed to do." For example, they may stilt their lovemaking by trying to do it "according to the book."

A first born married to a second born may often be uncomfortable. He/she must always be on guard against dethroning by his/her spouse. Therefore, a first born in this marriage may try to get approval and admiration rather than respect from the spouse. However, the quest may be in vain since the second born gives correction more easily than praise. Any attempt to make a favorable impression on the spouse, or on others, can bring humbling criticism from the spouse. The first born may simply be unable to pursue respect, admiration and approval in this marriage.

A first born will usually find marriage to a third born to be more pleasing than marriage to a second born. The third born is apt to grant the first born freedom to pursue approval and admiration from others and to ignore demands for respect without letting these demands bother him/her. However, if the third born should feel threatened by the first born, he/she may attack the first born's attempts at getting approval and admiration. The attack can confuse the first born, who may be unable to comprehend how getting approval and admiration from others could be worthy of the spouse's criticism. This marriage deteriorates further as the first born becomes more defensive and the third born becomes more aggressive. If the third born should be unable to induce changes in the first born, he/she may resort to other strategies in order to feel secure. The first born may discover, too late, that his/her third born spouse has made moves for self-protection that would leave him/her at a disadvantage if the marriage were to dissolve.

A first born may provoke a third born spouse to anger by ignoring, rejecting or belittling his/her ideas. However, the third born's anger will tend to be directed toward the first born's attention seeking rather than toward the first born's reaction to his/her ideas. By this misdirected anger the third born conceals his/her vulnerability. Consequently, the first born may never realize how he/she has angered the third born.

A first born married to a fourth born may miss the admiration, approval or respect he/she craves. Rather than admire the first born, the fourth born may be overly dependent on the first born, or try to control the first born. Consequently, the first born is apt to seek approval and admiration strokes more fervently from other people. For example, a first born husband may take to stopping at the bar on his way home, participate in hobbies that may take him away, or spend more time at work than is necessary. A first born wife, similarly, may belong to organizations, take on extra work or spend more time with friends than is necessary. These behaviors enable the first born to escape the fourth born's control and to obtain attention from others.

A first born may be most compatible with an only child. He/she may perceive the only child spouse's attempts to do right as respect. Furthermore, since the only child adult often enjoys time at home alone, the first born may be able to spend more time away from home with less complaint than with persons of other birth orders. On the negative side, this couple may have trouble developing closeness because both tend to avoid it for their own reasons. The first born will avoid intimacy in favor of approval, admiration and respect and the only child will avoid it to keep from feeling smothered.

SECOND BORN MARRIAGES

Although a second born married to a first born may feel inadequate when the first born attempts to impress others, he/she may feel most frustrated by the first born's tendency to leave out details. The second born, in his/her perfectionism, almost compulsively needs to possess the smallest details in order to feel adequate. When the details are not forthcoming, the second born may either try to dethrone the first born or become depressed. However, the first born, rather than the second born, is usually the more uncomfortable in this relationship.

Two second borns, married to each other, will tend to live rationally. Since both will probably be avoiding feelings in favor of logic, they may experience life as cut and dried. Life may be orderly, but not satisfying, without the richness of emotional contact.

Married to a third born, a second born may find criticism to have little effect on his/her spouse. In fact, the second born may become frustrated by the third born's ability to shrug off criticism. When the third born says "it doesn't bother me any," the second born knows he/she is not getting through. When the third born walks away from arguments rather than fight, the second born may feel helpless. The second born's strategies simply may not work with the third born. If, by chance, the second born should be able to corner the third born, he/she is apt to be told to do whatever he/she thinks is right. Thus, the second born discovers the third born to be perfectly capable of countering his/her strategies. Consequently, marriage to a third born can be trying for the second born.

A second born may be compatible to a fourth born spouse, especially during the early years of marriage. The second born's reliance on logic may give the fourth born a sense of security while the childlike stance of the fourth born may allow the second born to feel adequate. However, the second born may feel threatened later by the fourth born's increasing maturity.

Marriage to an only child may be the most difficult for a second born. The second born tends to feel frustrated by the illogical, i.e., emotional, response of the only child to his/her reasoning. Unable to induce the only child to accept his/her logic, the second born may try to exclude the only child from his/her plans, goals or work. In turn, the only child may stop communicating with the second born.

When the only child spouse stops communicating, the second born feels the loss of detail his/her spouse used to share. Trying to bring about change by criticizing the spouse can alienate the spouse even further. In this relationship, it appears that the only child spouse usually suffers more than the second born.

THIRD BORN MARRIAGES

More than any other birth order, third borns tend to adjust to the behavior of a spouse. Although it might thus appear that third borns make the best marriage partners, there can be problems. These problems arise from the third born's feelings of vulnerability and emotional attachment to his/her own ideas.

Married to a first born, the third born may inadvertently invite the spouse to push him/her into emotionally threatening situations by being passive. If the third born allows the first born to believe that nothing bothers him/her, he/she may find the first born planning his/her activities. However, these plans may create fear in the third born. Consequently, he/she faces the dilemma of confessing the fear or of participating in the activity. Feeling compelled to choose either option may create severe discomfort for the third born, who may solve the dilemma by attacking the spouse. Sometimes, a third born may suffer emotionally by trying to suppress fear while forcing himself/herself to do what the first born spouse wants.

A third born married to a second born appears to be comfortable in spite of the second born's critical ways. Having coped with a second born throughout childhood, the third born has learned to let the second born's criticisms roll off without ruffling him/her. In fact, a third born may find the second born's negative remarks amusing.

Two third borns, married to each other, may find life to be punctuated by a series of angry explosions which they trigger in each other. When one tries to share a new idea, the other may be preoccupied with his/her own ideas. The apparent disregard for his/her ideas can provoke the third born's anger, which the other will resent. Between explosions, the marriage can be serene.

A third born may find marriage to a fourth born to be difficult. He/she will probably discover that the fourth born knows how to cope with a third born's ways. Therefore, the third born may find his/her strategies, which work well with other people, simply will not work with the fourth born spouse. For example, if the third born tries to encourage the fourth born to be more outgoing, empathetic or courageous, the fourth born may pull into an emotional shell where he/she is impervious to the third born. Since a third born tends to feel rejected when his/her ideas are rejected, the third born spouse of a fourth born can feel unloved.

A third born may find marriage to an only child spouse to be more compatible. The third born will tend to adapt to the only child rather than try to change this self-directed person. However, the third born may create discomfort for the only child spouse by an excessive use of humor, which the spouse finds irritating because it often suggests he/she has not done something right. Furthermore, a third born may irritate an only child spouse by behaving unpredictably.

FOURTH BORN MARRIAGES

Fourth borns tend to operate from a sense of fear in their marriages.

A fourth born, married to a first born, may meet the first born's demand for respect passively, hoping the first born will let up. However, the fourth born's passivity may encourage the first born to continue efforts to get respect or to turn away from the spouse to get approval and admiration from others. If the first born spouse does turn to others for attention, the fourth born may cope by trying to control the spouse. Driven by fear, the fourth born may be unable to comprehend that trying to control the spouse's behavior may alienate the spouse even more. The feeling of immaturity can hinder the fourth born from adopting better strategies.

A fourth born may find marriage to a second born to be the most compatible. Since the second born may be occupied with overcoming the feeling of inadequacy, the fourth born may not be threatened by pressures from him/her. Moreover, if the second born criticizes, the fourth born may perceive it as an affirmation of his/her maturity. Therefore, the fourth born may feel accepted when corrected by the second born spouse.

A fourth born, married to a third born, may find that his/her strategies can alienate the third born. To his/her frustration, the fourth born may be unable to evoke the kind of response from the third born spouse he/she would like. In other words, the fourth born would like to have the third born accept him/her rather than just give permission to do whatever he/she wants to do. On the other hand, the fourth born is able to shrug off what the third born says without letting it get to him/her. If this marriage ends, the fourth born may be puzzled about the break-up and blame the spouse.

Two fourth borns married to each other may experience a marriage which is compatible when everything goes well. When difficulty develops, each may wait for the other to take the initiative to meet the difficulty. Quite often, the worse things get, the less they say to each other.

A fourth born may find marriage to an only to be the most difficult because he/she may not like the feedback from the only. The fourth born may find the blaming, which an only child can often do easily, to be very painful. The fourth born may also be frustrated to find that the spouse does not listen, but rather expects him/her to listen.

ONLY CHILD MARRIAGES

The only child may find marriage to a first born to be fairly compatible. The only child may satisfy the first born by respecting the spouse in the same way he/she respected parents as a child. The only child will tend to experience freedom as the first born seeks praise rather than trying to run the details of the only child's life. The only child may, however, find it difficult to relate as closely to the first born as he/she would like.

Although initially drawn to a second born, the only child may find marriage to a second born to be the most difficult. An only child is often attracted by a second born's dependability which makes him/her feel loved. However, the only child may discover that marriage to a second born can be very painful. The second born's logic, which may not have been so apparent before marriage, can become intolerable correction after marriage. Hurting from the second born's criticism and logic, the only child may eventually withdraw from the marriage. When the only child leaves the marriage, he/she may do it suddenly, before the second born can dissuade the only through logic. Once having escaped the marriage, the only child may be very reluctant to go back into the relationship.

The only child married to a third born may feel life to be tumultuous. The only child's desire for an orderly life may be threatened by the third born's tendency to take risks which appear unreasonable. The only child is likely to feel the fear which the third born denies for himself/herself.

The only child married to a fourth born may also find marriage to be difficult. The independent ways of the only child may threaten the fourth born, who may respond by trying to control the only child. The only child can feel quite smothered by the controlling behavior of the fourth born, but be unable to induce the fourth born to let up. As the only asserts his/her independence, the fourth born may, out of fear, try even harder to control the only child.

Two onlies married to each other may enjoy privacy since both of them crave time alone. On the other hand, this couple may not communicate well since each tends to talk without listening to the other. Their relationship may appear awkward, as they try to live together in separate worlds.

CONCLUSION

Fortunately, a couple can turn an unhappy marriage into a more satisfying, fulfilling and enjoyable relationship. By understanding the birth order effect on their marriage, they can develop more satisfying ways of relating to each other while avoiding behaviors which may offend the other. Furthermore, understanding that birth order, rather than sheer perversity of the spouse, has caused problems, a couple may feel encouraged to seek professional help for their marriage.

Birth Order in Parenting

Parents tend to interact with their children according to the dictates of their own birth order and those of their children.

Before looking at particular parent-child relationships, a general observation is in order. While sex does not seem to play a role in birth order development, children do appear to relate to parents according to sex. In relating to parents, a child will usually take the parent of the same sex as a role model and the parent of the opposite sex as a director. To do this, a child will WATCH the parent of the same sex and LISTEN to the parent of the opposite sex. Accordingly, a child will pattern his/her behavior on the parent of the same sex and develop his/her self-concept according to the feedback from the parent of the opposite sex.

In single parent families, a child usually fulfills the need for a role model or director through other adults with whom he/she has contact.

Parents tend to act as role models or give feedback according to their own birth orders. Children tend to respond to parental modeling and guidance according to their birth orders.

THE FIRST BORN PARENT

The first born parent tends to require respect of the children rather than seek their love. Consequently, if a child does not show respect, this parent may use punishment as a means of exacting respect from the child. Furthermore, this parent may enforce respect from the children for the other parent as well as for himself/herself.

Having a first born parent of the opposite sex tends to reinforce the first born characteristics of the oldest chld. Listening to this parent, the child tends to intensify his/her own first born attitudes. Furthermore, this first born child may develop positive self-esteem based on being first born since the first born parent is likely to approve or admire first born behavior.

If the first born parent of the same sex should be extreme in demanding respect, he/she may push the child into a second born position psychologically. In this case, the parent becomes more a sibling than a role model for the child. Therefore, the child may choose to be different from the parent by adopting second born strategies.

The first born parent, whose spouse feels victimized by the children, may try to rescue the spouse by forcing the children to respect the spouse. In this situation, a first born child may rebel if he/she is also trying to get respect rather than give it. In fact, a first born child may assume authority in a family in which a parent is unable to exercise it.

Unfortunately, first borns like to compare behaviors. Therefore, a first born parent may increase the feeling of inadequacy in the second born child by comparing this child's performance to that of others. By talking about how well he/she did as a child, or by highlighting other children's behavior, this parent can dishearten the child. Rather than encouraging the second born child to compete, these comparisons may cause the child to feel hopelessly condemned to inadequate performance. However, if the parent of the same sex makes the comparisons, the second born child may learn to use comparisons as a strategy to create feelings of inadequacy in others.

Feeling inadequate, the second born may perform very poorly. Consequently, being unable to encourage the child to do better, a parent may settle for mediocre performance by telling him/her to "just do the best you can." Instead of accomplishing its purpose, this statement may deepen the feeling of inadequacy because this child can interpret "doing the best you can" as requiring perfection. Therefore, it is better to encourage a second born to perform more adequately by saying "do what you can" rather than "do the best you can."

Of all the children in the family, a first born parent may have the severest conflicts with the third born child. Trouble develops when the third born child demonstrates that he/she is unafraid of the first born parent. Redoubling his/her efforts to get respect from this child escalates the conflict between them. Carried to an extreme, this conflict can cause the third born to resist all authority, an attitude which seems to get them into more trouble than children of other birth orders. With this child, it is very important for the first born parent of the opposite sex to aside his/her demands for respect in favor of being fair.

The third born child may adopt the respect-seeking ways of a first born parent of the same sex by becoming opinionated to keep others at a distance. This child would not use the parent's strategies to get respect, since respect is not a concern, but rather as a way to achieve emotional security.

The first born parent of a fourth born child is apt to treat this child more casually than he/she treats the other children. Usually, parents have mellowed with experience by the time they are raising the fourth child. Furthermore, since the fourth born child tends to be passive, the first born parent may not see a need to require respect of this child. On the other hand, this child, having seen the conflict between the first born parent and the other children, may give respect out of fear. In fact, observing conflicts between parents and older siblings can create lasting anxiety in the fourth born.

As an adult, the fourth born child, who models after a first born parent, may become extreme in demanding respect. Having to "try hard" by virtue of being fourth born, this child will try to outdo the parent. However, since his/her birth order does not support the demand for respect, the fourth born may vacillate between being stern and being passive.

The first born parent of an only child may not experience much conflict with this child, since this child often gives respect to the first born parent just to keep this parent from interfering with his/her life. In modeling after the parent, this child has ample opportunity to experiment with various adaptations of the parental model with imaginary companions. This child tends to process rather than adopt a parent's ways of behaving.

THE SECOND BORN PARENT

The second born parent brings both the feeling of inadequacy and the desire for perfection to the task of parenting.Feeling inadequate, this parent may interfere with the attention-seeking ways of the first born child to the point of making it difficult for this child to inspire admiration or respect in others. Admiration can be difficult to achieve if the parent does not permit the child to do something or have something which could bring admiration from peers. The parent may justify controlling and limiting this child as a way to keep him/her from shaming others who cannot perform well. In other words, a second born parent may try to protect other children from the arrogance of the first born.

Subconsciously feeling inadequate, the second born parent may correct the oldest child without giving significant compliments. Without positive feedback, especially from the parent of the opposite sex, a first born may despair of doing anything praiseworthy. On the other hand, if the first born thinks he/she can please a second born parent of the opposite sex, he/she may embrace perfectionism. However, this child's goal will be to impress others with perfect performance rather than to overcome a feeling of inadequacy in the manner of the second born parent. Consequently the first born's perfectionism will tend to be sporadic.

The frequent correction by a second born parent can create depression in the first born child, especially if it comes from the parent of the opposite sex. This child can develop a self-image of never being able to do well enough to satisfy others. Consequently, this child may perceive the world as demanding more than he/she can possibly deliver.

The second born parent is usually compatible with a second born child. The child will usually model after the second born parent of the same sex, unless the behavior of that person appears to be undesirable to this child. The feedback from the second born parent of the opposite sex would appear to make sense to this child.

The second born parent may find the third born child unruffled by anything he/she might say to this child. The third born child has learned to let the second born remarks roll off without being affected by them. Therefore, a third born child will probably not rebel toward a second born parent as he/she would toward a first born parent. The negative feedback of the second born parent is easier to ignore than the authority exercised by the first born parent. By ignoring the negative feedback of the second born parent of the same sex, the third born intensifies his/her own birth order characteristic of not letting anything bother him/her.

The third born child may model after a second born parent of the same sex by becoming critical, but for the purpose of keeping others at a distance. While the second born parent may be trying to feel adequate, the third born child is trying to feel safe.

The second born parent of a fourth born child may be very solicitous of the fourth born, since he/she does not threaten the second born's feeling of adequacy. If the parent is of the opposite sex, the fourth born child may respond by trying hard to do perfectly or by giving up out of frustration. If the suggestions of the second born parent are too much for the fourth born, this child may retreat into the feeling of immaturity by deciding to not care what he/she does.

If the second born parent is of the same sex, the fourth born may adopt the critical ways of the second born parent, but apply them inconsistently. The fourth born will tend to be critical when trying to feel grown up and passive when feeling immature. In other words, the fourth born child of a second born parent of the same sex will tend to vacillate between criticizing and withdrawing, according to his/her mood of the moment.

The only child will often react the most negatively to a second born parent of the opposite sex. Since the only child tends to feel angry at being corrected, this child will feel especially angry toward the frequent correction or criticism of the second born parent. The conflict escalates as the second born parent redoubles efforts to correct the only child, who reacts with even more anger.

If the second born parent of the only child is of the same sex, the child may adopt the critical ways of the parent in order to do things right. However, this child will use criticism to keep others from interfering in his/her life rather than to achieve feeling of adequacy.

THE THIRD BORN PARENT

The third born parent can be the kindest, most understanding and patient parent. The usual third born characteristics of refusing to let things bother him/her, and the feeling of empathy for children, can enable the third born parent to make his/her children feel loved, accepted and comfortable. Exceptions can occur, of course, if the third born parent experienced a traumatic childhood or is under stress.

Problems can occur when the third born's ways are opposed by the spouse. For example, a first born spouse may resent the third born's apparent acceptance of their children's disrespectful behavior. A second born spouse may object to the freedom the third born wants to give the children. A fourth born spouse may compete with the children for the attention of the third born, resenting the attention he/she gives the children. An only child spouse may resent the third born for not helping to control the children.

Two third born parents will often grant a great deal of freedom, acceptance and empathy to their children. However, if the parents trigger angry explosions in each other, they may create anxiety for their children. This anxiety may cause the children to develop stronger birth order characteristics in order to feel secure.

In relating to a third born parent of the same sex, each child does it differently. A first born child may imitate the parent by adopting his/her easy-going ways. However, the first born child does it to obtain approval, admiration and/or respect. The second born child may adopt the parent's easy-going way in order to feel adequate. Furthermore, the second born child may convert the strategy into criticism of others who are not easy-going. The fourth born child may try hard to be easy-going, often failing at it. The only child may find the third born's permissiveness as incompatible with his/her own desires to control.

67

THE FOURTH BORN PARENT

Parenting may be difficult for the fourth born who, as a child, was usually not given the experience of caring for siblings. As a result, the fourth born may not be psychologically prepared for parenting. Rather, even as a parent the fourth born may feel like a child trying to be accepted by his/her siblings.

In trying to parent, the fourth born may go to extremes in serving, loving or disciplining, without regard for the actual needs of the child. Rather than use his/her own judgment, he/she may take cues from the spouse. For example, if the spouse gets upset with a child, the fourth born parent may punish the child for upsetting the parent. In fact, the fourth born parent may try to surpass the other parent in punishing, controlling, showing empathy or giving freedom.

The fourth born parent may make life difficult for the first born child. If the fourth born parent should subconsciously expect the first born to be more mature than he/she is, he/she may try to exchange places emotionally with the first born. He/she may try to make the child take on the parental role while the parent continues in a childlike role. Naturally, a child will tend to resent this excessive responsibility when he/she should be enjoying childhood.

On the other hand, a fourth born parent may resent the respect-seeking ways of the first born child, especially if he/she perceives them to be an attempt by this child to take charge. Therefore, in order to keep this child from getting the upper hand, the fourth born parent may use various forms of punishment, control and restriction. In so doing, the fourth born parent may appear to be cruel to the first born.

If feeling childlike, the fourth born parent may depend on the first born child to meet his/her own needs. Accordingly, the fourth born parent may confide personal problems to the child or may expect the child to assume parental duties. In extreme cases, a fourth born father may use a first born daughter to satisfy himself sexually. In trying to meet the fourth born parent's expectations, the first born child may become very domineering over the younger children. This domination may arise from the inner rage at being required to do parenting rather than enjoying childhood. Rather than fight the parent, this child may take out his/her rage on the younger children. Later, as the child matures, he/she may direct his/her rage toward the parent as well.

In sibling conflicts, the fourth born parent will tend to side with the younger child. From his/her own childhood experience this parent understands how it feels to be at the mercy of older siblings. However, children learn to take advantage of the parent's sympathy by provoking conflict with older siblings, knowing that fourth born Mom or Dad will punish the older child. Consequently, sibling conflicts tend to be frequent in this family. In an attempt to curtail the strife, a fourth born parent may punish the older children even more severely. However, rather than feel gratified when the older child is punished, the fourth born child in this family may feel guilty. After all, he/she caused the older child to be punished. Later, as an adult, this person may continue to feel guilty whenever he/she has caused someone else to feel hurt. Furthermore, a fourth born may become sensitive to blame because of underlying guilt.

On the positive side, the child-like character of the fourth born parent may enable this parent to have rapport with the children. This parent can get down on the floor to romp with the children or have a heart to heart talk with a child. Thus, a fourth born parent may provide good companionship to children.

A fourth born, married to a first born, may be relegated to a position of being one of the chiildren. The fourth born may not be able to exercise power over the children since the first born may veto his/her decision. The fourth born parent in this situation may simply stop trying to parent.

The fourth born parent married to a second born may find parenting difficult if he/she is frequently corrected by the second born. If corrected consistently, the fourth born parent may become completely dependent on the second born parent to know what to do.

If the fourth born is married to a third born, he/she may reflect the parenting style of the third born by parenting kindly. Married to a third born, the fourth born can be a very understanding parent.

It is rare to find two fourth borns married to each other. As parents, they would probably experience great frustration, since they would try to push the parental role on each other. The children would probably exercise inordinate power over the parents in this family.

THE ONLY CHILD PARENT

The only child parent must learn to parent without having observed how his/her parents would do parenting with other children. Without this modeling, the only child parent may have to rely on imagination in order to do parenting. On the other hand, he/she may depend on the other parent to do the majority of the parenting.

While the only child may depend on the other parent, he/she may have trouble working in partnership with him/her. Having learned to do things alone, he/she will tend to leave the parenting to the spouse or do parenting alone, rather than work in cooperation. In this family, one parent will be in charge at a time if the only child has his/her way.

The only child parent with several children often tries to be completely fair with the children rather than treat them as individuals. For example, if one child needs shoes, this parent may buy shoes for all the children whether they

70

need them or not. If this parent does not have money to buy shoes for all the children, he/she may not get shoes for the one who does need them because "it would not be fair." Under this system, children learn to expect fairness, sometimes fighting with each other over what is fair.

The parental effort to be fair affects each child differently. The first born may resent not being given special consideration as the oldest. The second born may accept it as being logical. The third born may feel a lack of caring in mechanical fairness. The fourth born may feel included.

Birth Order
and Depression

Depression is a common psychological disorder which makes life miserable for many people. Though depression can have many causes, it may be helpful to understand how birth order strategies can cause depression.

For the purposes of this chapter, we will define depression as anger toward one's self. Accordingly, depression does not occur as long as a person can direct anger toward others. Whenever a person can no longer blame someone or something, anger may turn inward to become depression. For example, a person who divorces may become depressed after the divorce if the anger formerly directed toward the spouse becomes directed at the self.

Birth order strategies can lead to depression when a person realizes he/she has sacrificed too much while striving for a birth order dictated goal such as perfection, security or power. Furthermore, even if the person should achieve the goal, he/she may discover that the achievement does not satisfy as he/she expected. Consequently, he/she may become depressed for having pursued an objective which did not matter in the end.

FIRST BORN DEPRESSION

A first born may invite depression by pursuing approval, admiration and respect. These goals have a price. The first born may eventually come to know that, by striving for those kinds of attention, he/she turned away the very love he/she desired from friends and family. Having recognized his/her loss, the first born may become depressed for having traded unconditional love for momentary praise or grudging respect.

A first born who demands respect from his/her children may actually feel let down if the children give that respect. Subconsciously, a first born may prefer to be angry at not being respected to being happy at being respected. Consequently, receiving respect itself may be a step toward depression for the first born.

With persons outside the family circle, the first born may be laying the groundwork for depression by compromising too much in order to gain approval and admiration. Laying aside his/her own desires to accommodate others seldom accomplishes what the first born hopes. Whatever he/she gains by compromising usually does not compare to what he/she gives up. Accordingly, when the first born realizes how much he/she forfeited to please others, he/she may become depressed.

A first born may escape depression by choosing to value love over other kinds of attention. Accordingly, a first born needs to care for self rather than try to demand respect, grovel for approval or compete for admiration. In fact, by caring for self a first born may invite others to love him/her also. Love can be the antidote to depression for him/her.

SECOND BORN DEPRESSION

Second born depression tends to occur when the second

born has accomplished the task which he/she anticipated would make him/her feel adequate.

As long as a second born is striving to accomplish an objective, he/she can feel hopeful about future good feelings. While feeling hopeful, the second born can cover his/her feelings of inadequacy with dreams of coming triumphs. However, if success is achieved, the second born may be unpleasantly surprised to discover the feeling of inadequacy to be stronger than ever. Actually, he/she had conquered it only temporarily during the struggle for success. Since post-success depression appears to make no sense, it is often labelled as "burnout" and blamed on the hard work it took to achieve success.

The second born's strict goal orientation may create depression if other values are sacrificed. In moving toward success, he/she may have wiped out important relationships along the way. If the second born has alienated family and friends, he/she may come to feel isolated and lonely with achievement. The loneliness of success without love can generate depression.

Some second borns try to avoid feeling inadequate by changing occupations when on the verge of success, thereby always striving for a goal rather than achieving it. Other second borns fantasize about feeling adequate by accomplishing certain goals but do not strive for them. In other words, a second born may try to avoid depression by constantly striving but never arriving, or by not striving at all.

There is a better way. A second born may escape depression by placing more value on relationships than on accomplishments. Without giving up the skills he/she has developed, which may be considerable, a second born can include close relationships with other people in his/her life. A second born who permits self to have feelings for people along the way may also enjoy the goals he/she attains.

THIRD BORN DEPRESSION

Third born depression often occurs in the form of boredom.

Strategies used by a third born in overcoming vulnerability tend to make him/her feel bored. He/she may create boredom by turning away from people or situations which make him/her feel uneasy. He/she may create distance by attacking emotionally threatening persons or situations. He/she may create isolation by using religion as a shield against the insecurities of life. In other words, he/she may use various strategies to disengage from the uncomfortable aspects of life. By so doing, the third born may deprive himself/herself of satisfying relationships, isolate himeself/herself from interesting people, and hide from life behind a force-field of religion. Within these unnecessary sacrifices lie the seeds of depression for the third born.

The third born may escape depression by choosing to accept life with its risks rather than trying to make life absolutely safe. The acceptance of risks, especially in relationships, can make life stimulating, fulfilling and satisfying for the third born.

FOURTH BORN DEPRESSION

Fourth born depression often grows out of regret.

In coping with pressure, a fourth born may choose to ignore responsibilities imposed on him/her by others or by circumstances. Later in life, he/she may think back to what could have been if he/she had just cared more at the time. However, not caring is a defense mechanism, a mechanism which enables the fourth born to withdraw into a protective shell. Not caring is one way a fourth born handles unpleasant messages he/she does not want to hear.

For example, a fourth born may not care whether he/she finishes school, keeps a job, marries the right person, makes the right investment, gets a divorce, or achieves a particular goal. When, in retrospect, these things become significant for the fourth born, he/she may become depressed over what was lost by not caring.

To avoid depression, the fourth born needs to decide he/she does care about what is important. By recognizing he/she is going to lose by not caring, the fourth born may escape future depression by doing what is necessary now.

A fourth born may also experience depression when life becomes easy. As long as life feels difficult, the fourth born is able to overcome the feeling of immaturity by doing difficult things, hoping someday to feel grown up. When it is no longer necessary or possible to do difficult things, the fourth born may become depressed at feeling immature. When life becomes easy, the difficulties of life no longer offer protection to the fourth born from the feelings of immaturity.

The fourth born may, by complaining about having to endure life's difficulties, try to convince himself/herself, and others, that he/she is mature. Those who take fourth born complaints about life seriously may become confused when life improvement causes the fourth born to become more depressed. A difficult life may help a fourth born feel better by providing escape from the feelings of immaturity. Accordingly, a fourth born may try to assure himself/herself that life is difficult enough by complaining about it.

The fourth born may escape this depression by accepting himself/herself as mature enough. The fourth born needs to understand that maturity comes with age and experience, not from striving. With this understanding, a fourth born may be able to turn from courting difficulty to enjoying life as it is.

ONLY CHILD DEPRESSION

An adult only child may become depresed when he/she is finally been able to get things in order.

Although uncomfortable with disorder, an only child may garner good feelings by hoping that, someday, he/she will have life organized. When the only child finally achieves order, he/she may experience depression by missing the loved ones who had kept life unpredictable while they were there. Too late, the only child may discover that family, not orderliness, gives joy to life.

The only child may avoid depression by regarding disorder as a reminder that the people he/she loves are present. In relating to persons, as well as things, this birth order may escape depression and enjoy living.

An only child may also get depressed by being overwhelmed by work. Since an only child tends to stretch out the time taken for work and to shrink the time for play, he/she may feel that life is all work and no play. Consequently, he/she may become depressed at not being able to relax. To avoid this depression, the only child needs to separate work from play in his/her life. By separating the two, he/she may be able to work more efficiently and play more enjoyably and thus avoid depression.

CONCLUSION

This chapter is written to demonstrate links between birth order and depression. With this insight you may be able to create a happier life for yourself and others. However, this chapter is not meant to be a description of depression as a whole.

Depression can be a serious illness which needs professional attention. If you suspect someone is seriously depressed, get that person to a physician or other professional for help.

Communicating According to Birth Order

Your birth order position may hinder you from communicating productively with people. In fact, you may actually be blocking the very exchange you wish to nurture. However, by understanding what you do according to your birth order, you may be able to improve your communication with persons, to your benefit and their's.

Love is an important part of human relationships. Therefore, you may want to communicate love. However, if you fail to realize that people feel loved in different ways, instead of creating love you may cause dissatisfaction, unhappiness, or even hatred in others. Birth order theory may help you understand how you can help someone else, a spouse, child or friend, feel loved.

FIRST BORN COMMUNICATION

A first born may obstruct communication by trying to impress others. In trying to impress, the first born may appear to be arrogant, boastful and egotistical. Consequently, others tend to turn away from the first born rather than interacting with him/her.

Two first borns may feel awkward communicating with each other as they try to impress each other. Rather than listening to each other, they may compete with each other in trying to make the greatest impression. Communication may improve if one will set aside his/her desire to impress in favor of hearing and understanding what the other is saying.

In communicating with a second born, a first born may need to forego using personal illustrations which portray himself/herself in a favorable light. These illustrations only tend to make the second born want to dethrone a first born. Rather, the first born might communicate more effectively by sharing details with the second born.

In communicating with a third born, a first born's illustrations may trigger new ideas rather than admiration. If the first born will value these ideas rather than feel offended, he/she may enhance communication with a third born. However, if he/she shows irritation, the third born may simply withdraw.

To communicate effectively with a fourth born, a first born needs to embrace the fourth born as belonging. In other words, a first born needs to include the fourth born by using "we" rather than trying to impress by using "I." To do this, a first born needs to give up the attempt to obtain respect, admiration or approval from a fourth born.

To communicate effectively with an only, a first born needs to pay attention to the thoughts and feelings of the only before trying to promote his/her own ideas. Generally, an only finds the first born achievements to be uninteresting, except insofar as they impinge on his/her life. A first born who enables an only to get organized by sharing his/her plans, intentions, and desires, enhances communication with an only.

A first born may try to make others feel loved by giving them permission to do what they want. However, the giving of permission is an exercise of authority which others may reject. A second born may resent the permission as first born arrogance. A third born may find the permission humorously irrelevant to his/her behavior. A fourth born may feel belittled at the implication that he/she needs permission. An only may feel lost if the permission hides the first born's true feelings. Consequently, permission does not necessarily create feelings of being loved in any but another first born.

On the other hand, it can be difficult for others to make a first born feel loved. If given the opportunity, a first born will opt for other kinds of attention. However, there are two strategies which can help a first born feel loved.

Taking a first born by surprise can help a first born feel loved. The surprise element takes away the opportunity to exchange love for another form of attention. For example, a surprise party for a first born may make him/her feel loved, if he/she is not expecting this kind of attention. However, a planned party may encourage a first born to prepare himself/herself to be admired at the party. The feeling of being admired will take the place of feeling loved.

Another way to make a first born feel loved is to use a special form of communication in which a person gives admiration first, following it with an expression of caring. The admiration makes the first born receptive. Being receptive, he/she will usually accept the expression of caring, even if he/she becomes uncomfortable with it. Otherwise, the messages of caring might simply be rejected.

To make another first born feel loved, a first born needs to set aside his/her own desire for attention in order to give attention. Fortunately, being a first born may enable him/her to use the above strategies more easily.

A second born may feel great inner resistance to making a first born feel loved. His/her natural impulse is to undermine the arrogance of the first born. To make a first born feel loved, a second born needs to overcome the feeling of inadequacy. Otherwise, it might not be possible for a second born to give admiration or caring to a first born.

A third born may be the most creative in enabling a first born to feel loved. Once he/she understands what is necessary, he/she may create many new ways of helping the first born feel loved. Furthermore, since a third born may not feel threatened by a first born, the project may be enjoyable to the third born.

For a fourth born to make a first born feel loved, he/she has to become assertive enough to plan surprises and/or to communicate effectively. Fourth born passivity definitely blocks the ability to cause the first born to feel loved.

An only child may feel strong inner resistance to either surprising a first born or to giving admiration. An only child, not liking surprises, may not believe a first born could enjoy them either. As for admiration followed by caring, an only may fear inviting this person to intrude in his/her life. To help a first born feel loved, the only needs to accept the emotional risk involved.

SECOND BORN COMMUNICATION

Unlike the first born, who omits details, the second born emphasizes details in communication. When talking, the second born may try to get every detail right. When listening, the second born listens for details, especially the details that have been omitted by the speaker. By asking for details, the second born tends to make the first born uncomfortable, since he/she might come to know something that may detract from the first born's image. In fact, the first born may be apprehensive that an unforeseen detail may make him/her look bad.

Attention to detail may discomfort the other birth orders as well. The third born may feel vulnerable when the second born asks for details and bored when given all the details. A fourth born may feel blamed when asked for details and burdened when given all the details. An only child may feel intruded upon when details are requested and impatient when given all the details. Only another second born would probably feel comfortable in giving and receiving details on a regular basis.

Attention to detail can make the second born appear critical to persons of other birth orders. However, the second born tends to perceive himself/herself as being helpful, rather than critical, when suggesting improvements. The second born may not understand why someone else should feel offended by the "helpful suggestions" he/she wants to give.

The second born can improve communications by understanding the desires of others. With first borns, the second born may want to set details aside to view the big picture. With third borns, the second born may want to hold off making suggestions while considering his/her ideas. The second born may want to be aware that attention to detail could make a fourth born feel blamed. With the only child, the second born may want to avoid appearing intrusive by giving or asking for unncessary details.

A second born can also improve communication by paying attention to feelings as well as logic. When a spouse complains that the second born "is always right," the spouse is reacting to the second born's use of logic against his/her feelings. The spouse may be frustrated that the second born seems to be ignoring feelings.

A simple way to pay attention to feelings is to talk about likes and dislikes. For example, a second born could express pleasure at a first born's accomplishments, a third born's ideas, a fourth born's efforts and an only child's performance. He/she may be pleasantly surprised by the way people respond to this kind of communication.

Others can help a second born feel loved by giving him/her details. A first born can help a second born feel loved by setting aside the desire to present a favorable image in order to give the second born details about his/her activities. A third born may help a second born feel loved by taking the risk of feeling vulnerable by sharing the details a second born craves. A fourth born can take responsibility for how the second born feels by relating details. An only child can set aside the desire for privacy to confide the details of his/her life.

Two second borns will tend to make each other feel loved since they may naturally share details.

THIRD BORN COMMUNICATION

A third born often communicates in ways that keep others at a comfortable distance. A third born may do this by withdrawing from confrontation, by resorting to humor, and by generating ideas to act as a buffer between himself/herself and others. Sometimes a third born will use anger, especially if nothing else works, to maintain emotional space.

Withdrawing may cause problems for others. By withdrawing from confrontation, a third born can create guilt in the first born, a sense of inadequacy in the second born, helplessness in the fourth born and frustration in the only child. In other words, each person will tend to interpret the third born's withdrawal according to the dictates of his/her birth order position. However, another third born may perceive withdrawal as a natural response to stressful situations.

To communicate positively, a third born needs to set aside the desire for security to take his/her chances in relating to others. Rather than withdrawing from confrontation, the third born may want to risk conflict to work out differences. By so doing, a third born can enhance the possibilities for better relationships.

To improve relations with a first born, a third born may want to refrain from joking about a first born's feats. It is better to appreciate his/her achievements, even though appreciation might encourage a first born to seek more praise. The risk is worth the potential benefits of a good relationship.

Communication with a second born can be improved if the third born will give lots of details with the ideas he/she suggests. By so doing, the third born enables a second born to feel more adequate through knowing what the third born is thinking.

Communication with another third born may be enhanced by considering the other's ideas rather than yielding to the temptation to produce his/her own ideas.

This may be difficult since ideas tend to stimulate more ideas for a third born.

Communication with a fourth born may be improved if the third born takes care to include the fourth born in his/her ideas. By showing how the fourth born belongs, the third born may create positive feelings in him/her.

Communication with an only child may be improved if the third born gives this person time to digest new ideas. The only child needs time to reorganize his/her thoughts to incorporate fresh ideas. He/she could become frustrated if the third born pushes for responses too quickly or promotes novel ideas before the only child has dealt with the previous ones.

In spite of the tendency to fear close encounters, the third born may crave closeness. Those who understand the third born's feelings may enable this person to feel loved.

A first born may enable a third born to feel loved by setting aside his/her desire to impress in order to listen to the ideas of the third born. When a first born takes these ideas seriously and gives them value, the third born may feel loved.

A second born may enable a third born to feel loved by foregoing criticism in order to find positive value in the third born's ideas. A fourth born may enable a third born to feel loved by giving up the temptation to limit the third born's thinking. An only child may enable a third born to feel loved by listening to his/her ideas rather than projecting his/her own thoughts on them.

FOURTH BORN COMMUNICATION

Fourth borns often find communication to be difficult. As children, they often were ignored, patronized or rejected when they tried to communicate. Since there were at least five older persons with whom they had to compete in order to be heard, they often failed to get through to them. Sometimes, they would have to resort to screaming or hitting in order to compel others to listen.

As adults, fourth borns may continue to believe that no one will listen. Consequently, in trying to communicate they may speak more loudly than necessary, talk continually to keep others listening, or turn on their anger when conversing. Subconsciously, they may still believe they have to take special measures to be heard.

The fourth born's communication strategies may appear disrespectful to first borns, unnecessarily emotional to second borns, threatening to third borns and oppressive to onlies. While fourth born communication may seem appropriate to another fourth born, two fourth borns will tend to stop communicating when their relationship is under stress. They tend to listen as poorly as they believe other people listen.

Communication may improve when a fourth born recognizes that others will listen to him/her as they do to other adults.

A fourth born can communicate effectively to a first born if he/she cares about whhat the first born wants. By caring, the fourth born may connect with the first born's craving to be loved. However, the fourth born may need to perservere rather than withdraw when the first born appears more interested in being praised than in being loved. Persistence in caring may pay off in better communication.

A fourth born can communicate more effectively with a second born by making a special effort to include details. As a child, the fourth born may have had to speak briefly in order to finish before others lost interest in what he/she was saying. This very brevity, with its lack of detail, may cause the second born to stop listening. A fourth born can improve communication with a second born by taking the risk of going into detail.

A fourth born may improve communication with a third born by listening rather than trying to control. Controlling a third born may be tempting to the fourth born as a way to make the third born stay and listen. However, choosing to listen will usually work better because it is less threatening to the third born. In turn, a third born will be more likely to listen.

A fourth born may improve communication with another fourth born by listening carefully and thoughtfully. By listening, one fourth born may encourage another to communicate fully rather than briefly, and to talk rather than withdraw.

A fourth born may improve communication with only by paying attention to the only's feelings, attitudes and ideas before trying to communicate. With this prior attention, a fourth born may encourage an only to listen to him/her.

Others can help a fourth born feel loved. A first born can enable a fourth born to feel loved by setting aside his/her desire to impress in order to help the fourth born feel a sense of belonging. The desire to impress has the effect of alienating the one being impressed. Sacrificing praise in favor of including the fourth born may enable the fourth born to feel loved.

A second born may help a fourth born feel loved by turning from logic to feeling. Accordingly, a second born may give a hug to make the fourth born feel loved rather than trying to think for him/her.

A third born can help a fourth born feel loved by allowing himself/herself to be touched emotionally by the fourth born. The usual "it doesn't bother me" attitude of the third born can make the fourth born feel rejected. If a third born responds with feeling to a fourth born, the fourth born may feel accepted.

Two fourth borns can help each other feel loved by learning to listen to each other. As each discovers that the other listens, they may feel accepted and included by each other. In this mutual acceptance they may feel loved.

An only may encourage a fourth born feel loved by listening rather than projecting his/her own ideas. The only child attitude which says, "you are the way I think you are," tends to make the fourth born feel rejected. By setting aside his/her own assumptions to listen to the fourth born, the only may enable him/her feel loved.

ONLY CHILD COMMUNICATION

The only child tends to project his/her own perceptions on others, believing that others are the way he/she assumes them to be.

Therefore, the only often communicates as if the other person were what he/she projects. This kind of communication often misses the mark, making the other person feel misunderstood.

Projection creates various barriers to communication. For example, an only's projections may confuse the first born who may be out of touch with his/her feelings. The first born may believe the only's definition of him/her, trying to communicate with the only child accordingly. For example, if an only defines the first born as selfish, the first born may try to stop being selfish whether or not he/she is, in fact, selfish.

A second born may respond to the only's projection by marshalling evidence which contradicts it. Usually, the second born's logic inspires the only to try even harder to establish his/her projection as true. Thus, the struggle between them can escalate.

When defined by an only, a third born may examine himself/herself. He/she might ask others if they think that what the only said is true. In spite of trying to keep the only's assumptions from bothering him/her, the third born may feel vulnerable.

A fourth born usually meets an only's projection with flat denial. Having learned to reject projection as a child, the fourth born may not even consider whether there is truth in the only's assumptions.

Two onlies may try to project on each other. They may give the appearance of living in separate worlds, not truly comprehending each other. When communicating, they may meet each others' projections with projections of their own.

An only child can improve communication by learning to accept persons as they are. Setting aside assumptions, the only may enhance communication by becoming engrossed in how others think and feel. The only may discover that people like to be taken as they are, or as they see themselves to be. Moreover, the only may discover people to be very interesting when he/she truly comes to know them.

In order to feel loved, an only usually needs to be able to depend on others. Surprises may make an only feel uncomfortable, if not unloved. Therefore, an only may become annoyed with a first born who likes to create surprises. Surprising an only, even with a pleasant surprise, can have the effect of making the only feel unloved. To make an only feel cared for means keeping the only informed, being on time, and keeping promises. A first born may need to set aside his/her demand that an only respect his/her freedom in order to meet the only's need for dependability.

A second born can make an only feel cared for by responding to feelings. For example, a second born might say to an only, "You look angry," rather than asking, "What is wrong?" The former invites the only to talk about feelings, the latter to shift from feelings to making a report. Valuing the only's feelings can make the only feel loved.

A third born's creativity can make it difficult for an only to feel loved. His/her ideas, sudden changes in plans and unpredictable behavior can keep an only in an uncomfortable state of uncertainty. Therefore, a third born may help an only feel cared for by becoming predictable enough for the only to know what to expect.

A fourth born may help an only feel loved by becoming dependably assertive. When the fourth born becomes assertive, he/she may keep the only from making assumptions which may be detrimental to the relationship. Furthermore, a fourth born who is assertive enough to be reliable can enable an only to feel loved.

Since an only is often dependable, two onlies can make each other feel loved. However, since both tend to project on each other, they may have trouble making emotional contact with each other. Both need to set aside

Overcoming Limitations

Birth order strategies, which enabled a child to cope with life, often handicap the adult. While the adult might rely on birth order tactics to get along, he/she may be frustrated by their impotency in mastering life. Replacing these birth order strategies with more appropriate adult behaviors can add new dimensions to a person's existence. Birth order limitations can be overcome.

In the process of using birth order strategies, a person usually develops strength as well as limitations. Fortunately, even though a person conquers birth order limitations, he/she will usually retain these special strengths. For example, a first born, who becomes aware of his/her own feelings, can still continue to be aware of how others react. A second born, who achieves a feeling of adequacy, can still attend to details. Though he/she becomes assertive, a third born can still have empathy for others. A fourth born can overcome the feeling of immaturity while continuing to be able to work hard. An only, who comes to accept others as they are, can still retain his/her organizational ability. Rather than losing, a person who prevails over birth order limitations adds possibilities to his/her life.

A person creates his/her birth order position by making certain decisions as a child. Therefore, since birth order is created by decisions, he/she may be able to overcome birth order limitations by making new decisions. Sometimes, persons will make new decisions when they grasp the nature of birth order. However, specific questions can be helpful in provoking persons into making these new decisions.

This chapter includes some questions which challenge birth order. As you consider these questions, notice that they ask you to give yourself permission to do or feel something which is restricted by your birth order position. Consequently, you may experience inner resistance to answering the questions affirmatively. By the way, the "right" answer to each question is "yes."

The appropriate questions for your birth order can be helpful in making liberating decisions for yourself. Remember, if one set of questions does not seem to work for you, you may belong to a different birth order. Consequently, the questions which affect you may reveal your actual psychological birth order. Consider the possibility that your birth order position may be different than you had assumed.

FIRST BORN QUESTIONS

If you are first born, the following questions may challenge your birth order position. Consequently, they may touch you more deeply than you anticipate.

> Is is okay for you to be happy?
> Is it okay for you to put love ahead of respect?
> Is it okay for you to feel okay when you do not get respect?
> Is it okay for you to have what you want?

Is it okay for you to be happy? The answer may seem obvious, but if you are first born you may have trouble saying "yes." You may qualify your answer because you usually set aside your own desires in order to get attention from others. Ever since your birth order decision as a small child, you have felt it was not okay for you to be happy unless you considered others first. Unfortunately, since you are never done considering others, you may never have gotten around to being happy yourself. Consequently, you have hoped to become happy some day, rather than feeling happy right now. When you decide it is okay for you to be happy, you make happiness possible for yourself.

When you decide it is okay for you to be happy, you may become more aware of your own feelings. As a first born, you tend to suppress your own feelings in order to care for others' feelings. Consequently, you may experience your feelings as inconsistent, sporadic and compulsive. You may lose track of them. In fact, you may not even know how you feel until you know how someone else feels. Your feelings will tend to reflect how others feel rather than arise from within yourself. When you decide it is okay for you to be happy, you may be able to have your own feelings.

How does deciding it is okay for you to be happy make you more aware of your feelings? The answer lies in how the subconscious works. While you live out your birth order, your subconscious protects you by blocking out your feelings. Since you may not indulge your feelings, your subconscious saves you from having to face them. However, when you decide it is okay for you to be happy, your subconscious can be free to let you be aware of your feelings.

Is it okay for you to put love ahead of respect? Deciding it is okay for you to do so can markedly improve your relationships with family and friends. Your childhood decision to require respect of others may have led you to set aside the love you could have had. Consequently, you may have come to assume that your family did not care for you. However, when you decide it is okay to put love ahead of respect, you may discover that family and friends really do care about you. When you discover this love, you will, no doubt, find you are much more satisfied with it than you were with respect.

How do you put love ahead of respect? A part of you knows how. You know how to overlook things which others do. You know how to be gracious—you do it with persons outside the family. Giving yourself permission to put love ahead of respect may allow you to be gracious with family.

Is it okay for you to feel okay when you do not get respect? A part of you may resist this idea. However, you will not be free to choose love over respect as long as part of you feels angry at disrespect. Perhaps it would help if you were to believe that your family wants you to be human rather than exercise power over them. What you see as disrespct may, in fact, be an invitation for you to be human with them so they can love you.

Is it okay for you to have what you want? This question encourages you to decide you are worthy of having your desires fulfilled. Answering this question may help you overcome your compulsion to compromise your own inclinations in order to please others. You may finally be able to get what you want. Not only will you be able to get what you want, you may come to know what it is you do want.

As a first born, you tend to move whichever way the emotional wind blows. New decisions in response to the first born questions may enable you to set your own direction for your own life. Consequently, you may be able to move against the wind when you so desire.

SECOND BORN QUESTIONS

If you are second born, the following questions may

94

help you conquer some of your birth order limitations.

Is it okay for you to feel okay even if you do something imperfectly?

Is it okay for you to feel okay, even if everything is not perfect?

Is it okay for you to put feelings ahead of logic?

Is it okay for others to be the way they are?

If you are second born, the desire for perfect performance may limit what you can accomplish. While you are getting the details right, you may miss getting the major things right. You may win a lot of battles as you lose the war.

Is it okay for you to feel okay even if you do something imperfectly? You decided, as a child, that to feel okay you had to achieve perfection in something. By deciding it is okay for you to feel okay when you have done something imperfectly, you re-program that early decision. You give yourself permission to feel good even though every detail is not right in what you have done.

Perhaps even more importantly, you are giving yourself permission to take on tasks which cannot be done perfectly. You may be able to rise above a limited area of endeavor, in which you concentrate on details, to a wider area of endeavor in which you can focus on goals. You can lay aside the narrow brush which paints the details for the larger brush which paints a bigger picture.

Is it okay for you to feel okay even if everything is not perfect? As a second born, you will tend to notice imperfections in what others do, just as you notice them in your own performance. Consequently, you may offend others by frequently correcting their minor or insignificant faults. Allowing yourself to feel okay, even if everything is not perfect, enables you to overlook imperfections in what others do, enhancing your relationships with them. By overlooking inconsequential imperfections you may help create a friendlier environment for yourself and others.

Is it okay for you to put feelings ahead of logic? As a second born, you may choose logic over feelings because logic lends itself to perfection. Of course, there is no perfection in feelings. However, since relationships are often based on feelings, you may alienate others through excessive use of logic. You may be creating resentment or depression in the very people with whom you wish to be close.

You may be tempted to use logic by analyzing feelings. Unfortunately, you can analyze feelings to death. This may be useful for overcoming undesirable feelings, but harmful in handling desirable feelings. Therefore, to be happy, analyze your bad feelings but not your good feelings.

Even though you want to allow yourself to put feelings first, something in you may resist. A part of you may feel inadequate if you allow feelings to have precedence over logic. Nevertheless, for the sake of closer relationships, you may want to risk letting down the protective wall of logic.

Of course, life could be disastrous if you lived from feelings alone. At times, you must act out of logic. Therefore, you must realize you have not denied yourself the privilege of putting logic first when it is appropriate. You have simply given yourself the additional option of putting feelings first when you want.

Is it okay for others to be the way they are? This question invites you to accept others with their imperfections. You will probably discover that your relationships will be enhanced when you stop trying to perfect your friends. They are more likely to open up their thoughts, feelings and ideas to you when you cease trying to improve what they share with you. Letting others be the way they are may let you enjoy them rather than drive them away.

THIRD BORN QUESTIONS

If you are limited by third born strategies, you can expand your boundaries by answering the following questions.

Is it okay for you to take risks in relationships?
Is it okay for you to enjoy your fears?
Is it okay for you to be human instead of strong?
Is it okay for you to take chances?

Is it okay for you take risks in a relationship? As a third born you tend to take full responsibility for relationships by avoiding disagreements which may threaten the harmony of these relationships. By so doing, you may frustrate friends who want to work out differences with you. By sidestepping confrontation, you may harm relationships by refusing to take the necessary risks in working out these differences.

Is it okay for you to enjoy your fear? Strange as it may seem to you, it is possible to enjoy fear. Observe how people pay for the privilege of enjoying fear through carnival rides, skydiving, fright movies, racing cars and skiing. Many people enjoy the fear of encountering strangers, public speaking, gambling and starting new businesses.

If you enjoy your fear, fear becomes a motivation, a source of energy, and a means of being alert. On the other hand, if you are afraid of fear, you may find yourself paralyzed by it. If you try to suppress your fear, you may find it overwhelming as it gathers strength from being suppressed. Enjoy your fear, and it could be an ally to you.

Is it okay for you to be human rather than strong? You may trying to rise above being human by being so strong nothing can bother you. This pedestal is a slippery place from which you may often slide into the pit, where you feel yourself to be weak. Consequently, your real strength lies in being human, rather than in trying to be strong.

Is it okay for you to take your chances? To others you may appear to be taking many risks, but within yourself you may be denying the reality of risk. You may be convincing yourself that nothing bad can happen to you. Yet, you know that anything that happens to human beings could happen to you. By deciding it is okay for you to take your chances as a human being, you relieve yourself of the burden of trying to conquer the feeling of vulnerability in a world where everyone is vulnerable. Your decision may enable you to give up the fear of fear itself.

FOURTH BORN QUESTIONS

If you are fourth born, you may experience liberation by responding affirmately to the following questions.

Is it okay for you to be grown up?
Is it okay for you to do things the easy way?
Is it okay for you to care?
Is it okay for you to put logic ahead of fear?

As a fourth born, you tend to act either passively or aggressively with people. On the one hand, since you were excluded as a child, you may tend to withdraw from challenges. On the other hand, having had to use force to be heard as a child, you may tend to become aggressive with others, especially family members. These questions will tend to challenge both your passive and aggressive behaviors.

Is it okay for you be grown up? As a fourth born, you may feel that everyone, perhaps even your own child, is bigger, stronger, and more capable than you are. You have trouble feeling grown up. To overcome this feeling, you may need to decide it is okay for you to be grown up. Perceiving yourself as an adult may help you feel grown up.

Is it okay for you to do things the easy way? You may not want to say "yes" because the easy way may appear to you as laziness, sloppiness or immaturity. For you to feel grown up, you may feel that you must do things the hard way, even though you could accomplish as much or more the easy way.

You may need to understand that, with maturity, tasks that were difficult become easier. By deciding it is okay for you to do things the easy way, you tend to accept yourself as a mature adult who is capable of doing difficult tasks easily.

Is it okay for you to care? As a means of self-defense, you may have adopted an "I don't care" attitude toward anything which felt oppressive. For example, if someone criticized you, you may have chosen to not care how he/she felt about what you did. You may even have decided to not care if things went badly for you. In fact, you may have decided to care less and less as things got worse and worse. Obviously, not caring can bring on serious consequences in your life. Therefore, to make your life work, you may want to decide it is okay for you to care.

Is it okay for you to put logic ahead of fear? As a fourth born, fear could drive you to excessive monitoring of your child's behavior, extreme dependence on a spouse or other person, or into passivity or aggressiveness in relationships. Deciding it is okay to put logic ahead of fear may enable you to conquer this birth order behavior. For example, logic may enable you, as a parent, to grant reasonable freedom to your child, even though fear may make you want to control him/her.

As a fourth born child, you may have adopted a clam-like strategy of withdrawal or a crab-like strategy of attack. At times, you may wait like a clam for life to bring you what you want. At other times, like a crab, you may attack others to get what you want. Consequently, when you live out of your birth order, you may find it difficult to participate reasonably in life. Answering these questions affirmatively may enable you to adopt better strategies for living.

ONLY CHILD QUESTIONS

If you are an only child, the following questions may help you expand the dimensions of your life.

> Is it okay for you to do what you want, even when you do not feel like it?
> Is it okay for you to do what you feel like doing, when you want?
> Is it okay for you to take the chance of making a mistake?

Is it okay for you to do what you want, even when you do not feel like it? As an only, you may be confused by the apparent distinction between "wanting" and "feeling." You may take them to be identical. Therefore, it may not make sense for you to "want" to do something you do not "feel" like doing.

Though you do not distinguish between "wanting" and "feeling," you may distinguish between "wanting" to do something and "having" to do something. Accordingly, anything you do that you do not feel like doing is something you "have" to do. Essentially, you perceive yourself as a slave who is forced to perform onerous tasks against his/her will.

This question can set you free. To understand the meaning of this question, you need to realize that when you do what you do not feel like doing, you are behaving responsibly. As an adult, you are doing what you "want" to do when you do something you do not "feel" like doing. This change of perception from "having" to do things to "wanting" to do things may enable you to move from being a victim of circumstances to taking charge of your life.

Deciding it is okay to do what you want to do, even if you do not feel like it, implies there is nothing you "have to" do. However, there are those things you want to do that make life work for you. You will want to do these things whether or not you feel like it. When you realize you want to do them, you may perceive yourself as a self-disciplined, responsible person.

Is it okay for you to do what you feel like doing when you want? As an only, you may have trouble enjoying yourself because you keep thinking about things you "have to" do. This question challenges you to give yourself permission to lay aside your responsibilities in order to enjoy yourself by doing what you feel like doing. However, by doing it when you want, you choose to do it responsibly rather than indulging yourself to the detriment of other aspects of your life.

Since you are challenging a birth order strategy, you may find yourself resisting the idea of doing what you feel like doing when you want. Despite the discomfort of being a "slave" to chores, you may find it difficult to say "yes" to pure enjoyment. Yet, you will only find the time to enjoy yourself when you actually allow yourself to do what you feel like doing when you want.

As an only, you may need to separate work from play. When you are doing the work you want to do, you need to put on your work hat. When you are doing what you feel like doing, you need to put on your play hat. By separating the two, you are more likely to work effectively and to play delightfully.

Is it okay for you to put logic ahead of feelings? As an only, you tend to react to persons emotionally rather than rationally. For example, when someone discusses an idea with you, you may react by telling him/her how you feel about the idea rather than thinking about it rationally. By allowing yourself to put reason ahead of feeling, you may be able to enhance your relationships with others.

When you decide it is okay to put logic ahead of feelings, you simply give yourself a new option. You can still put feelings ahead of logic when you want to do so. Of course, it will be appropriate for you, at times, to put feelings ahead of logic.

Is it okay for you to take the risk of making a mistake? Your early decision to do things right may limit you to doing only those things you know you can do correctly. You may avoid doing these things in which you may err, thereby restricting your opportunities to grow, learn and experience. When you decide it is okay for you to risk making mistakes, you may discover many more possibilities in your life.

The only child questions encourage you to take charge of your life. As an only, you may have lived as if other people and external circumstances ruled your life. You may have felt constantly victimized, unable to ever feel free. These questions invite you to experience freedom by seeing yourself as the manager of your life.

The Future of Birth Order

The day may come when birth order consultants will be used in industry, education, entertainment, business, crime prevention, mental health, communications and religion. These consultants may help clients to handle themselves better, improve their communications, and accomplish their goals. They may not only assist their clients, they may create better relationships between everyone involved.

Why use a birth order consultant? Birth order can help identify the dynamics of interaction. It may help provide a framework by which a person can understand how people relate to each other. It may take the mystery out of human behavior for the average person. Most importantly, it may suggest how beneficial changes can be made.

Let's look at some areas in which birth order knowledge may be helpful.

COMMUNICATIONS

Birth order consultants may someday give guidance to those who communicate to others. A consultant may be especially valuable to a client who communicates to an occupational group in which one or two birth orders predominate.

Many groups do tend to be composed of a particular birth order. For example, clergy tend to be first born, bankers second born, salespeople third born, and managers fourth born. Taking into consideration the birth order characteristics of a group may greatly enhance the effectiveness of advertising, publications and direct communication to the group's members.

Even when dealing with a homogeneous group, birth order may suggest strategies for improving communications. For example, consider how a first born pastor may experience difficulty with a congregation. The very manner in which he/she tries to impress the congregation may cause second borns to want to bring down the pastor. Without realizing it, the first born clergy may have created unnecessary conflict within the congregation. Knowing birth order might help first born clergy to avoid the pitfalls and to inspire the people, including second borns. Someday, a consultant may help clergy do just that.

Anyone who wants to communicate to people needs to recognize his/her own birth order limitations in order to transcend them in speaking or writing. The person communicating also needs to understand how persons of other birth orders process information.

EDUCATION

Birth order consultants may one day enable teachers to teach more effectively. Through understanding the birth order characteristics of their children, teachers may be able to help each child individually according to his/her ways of coping. By understanding their own birth orders, teachers may be able to use a greater variety of teaching strategies.

A teacher may learn to like children whom he/she has disliked because of birth order differences. For example, the second born teacher may be able to enjoy the first born child, if the teacher understands the child's seeking of approval and admiration as a birth order characteristic. Recognizing the birth order differences, a teacher may be able to motivate children much more effectively than his/her birth order position would normally permit. The results could be pleasing for both teacher and student.

EMPLOYMENT

Those who employ persons in their business may find the greatest immediate payoff in dollars and cents by using birth order information. The day may come when employees will use birth order consultants on a regular basis for guidance in working with employees.

Knowing birth order can make performance on the job more predictable. An employer can deploy his work force effectively if he/she knows that first borns work best with people, second borns with detail, third borns with selling, fourth borns with management and onlies with organization. Using birth order may enable an employer to avoid painful and costly mistakes with employees.

For example, an employer may want to consider very carefully whether or not to promote a third born salesman to the position of sales manager, where he could become unproductive. If the employer knows that the salesman's third born characteristics make him a good salsman, he/she may want to keep him in sales rather than use him ineffectively in management.

A birth order order consultant may help an employer understand why first borns might cater to people without benefit to the business, why second borns might irritate customers, why third borns might take unnecessary risks, why fourth borns might make work difficult, and why onlies might get upset with unexpected changes. Instead of having to either tolerate the employee's behavior or discharge him/her, the employer may be able to use the employee in a more suitable capacity.

COUNSELING

Since birth order theory was developed in a counseling setting, it may be especially useful for counselors in diagnosing and treating their clients' behaviors. Knowing a client's birth order can enable a counselor to begin therapeutic interaction quickly. Knowing his/her own birth order characteristics may enable the counselor to develop new strategies to meet the needs of clients, and to discard ineffective strategies.

Sharing birth order information can make the counseling session educational for clients. By so doing, a counselor may help a client make changes more rapidly and thoroughly. The counselor may also give his/her client a life-changing perception of himself/herself and others through birth order.

Birth order may become an important element in counseling training in the future. It may provide a structure by which many characteristics of human behavior might be understood.

CRIME

Understanding birth order effects may save money, human resources and emotional pain for society by defining strategies that can help people, especially the young, to turn from crime to productive living.

Those who commit crimes may be carrying out birth order strategies which serve them in their particular setting. For example, first borns may get admiration from peers and fourth borns may feel a sense of belonging by engaging in crime. Rehabilitation strategies which take into account the individual's birth order may enable society to rehabilitate offenders.

Understanding third born behavior may pay the greatest dividends in fighting juvenile crime. Knowing how third borns can feel compelled to demonstrate their fearlessness may allow society to deal more effectively with them. Helping parents and teachers understand third born behavior may enable them to redirect these children before they come to the attention of the law.

The day may come when legal systems, especially those dealing with young offenders, may use birth order to develop appropriate interventions to turn them from crime.

MOTIVATION

Most motivational efforts in our society seem to be directed toward third borns. They appeal to third borns through an emphasis on emotional and mental strength. Consequently, third borns tend to follow through on such motivational efforts while others tend to lose interest quickly even though they may become enthusiastic at first. If everyone is to be motivated, it must be understood that people are motivated according to their birth orders. First borns tend to be motivated by the opportunity to help or impress others. Second borns are usually motivated by the challenge to achieve. Third borns may be moved by the call to self-discipline which promises personal power. Fourth borns might be moved by difficulty. Onlies may relish the freedom to organize things their own way. By considering birth order, motivational efforts can be tailored to effectively inspire everyone for a longer period of time.

Birth order may provide new dimensions to motivational efforts of the future. Programs may be designed to motivate specific groups according to their birth order characteristics. General motivational programs may include motivators for all birth orders.

ENTERTAINMENT

Television dramas may be able to interest more people, have greater emotional impact and involve viewers more fully by incorporating birth order concepts.

If the characters of a drama were to conform to birth order characteristics, they could become more realistic to the audience. People would tend to react to these characters as they do to people in real life. Each person viewing a drama could identify with characters having the same birth order. He/she could also react to other characters according to compatibility or incompatibility with their birth orders. The viewer's involvement in the drama would be more complete, emotionally and mentally.

Birth order analysis may help writers by suggesting new interactions for the characters. For example, by including all five birth orders in the characters of a script, writers could develop fifteen different scenarious using just two characters at a time. Adding more characters multiplies the possibilities of dramatic interaction.

Birth order analysis can establish the rules of behavior for each character according to the birth order assigned to that person. As the writers become familiar with these rules, they may bring these characters to life more easily.

By understanding their own birth order limitations, writers can get beyond them in creating behavior for the characters they create. Otherwise, each character may simply be acting out different versions of the writer's own birth order characteristics.

POLITICS

By utilizing birth order, politicians running for office can improve their chances of winning elections by improving their communication. Not only may they be able to communicate better, they may also be able to alter their own birth order behaviors which tend to create negative reactions in other birth orders. Overcoming personal limitations will pay dividends for the politician when he/she speaks off the cuff in debates, answers questions and participates in informal gatherings. At those times, the politician who understands birth order can communicate most effectively. The more thoroughly the politician understands and controls his/her birth order characteristics, the better image he/she can project to others.

Especially important to politicians may be the ability to communicate to only children, who constitute a large percentage of the population. Normal birth order communication styles do not speak to the only child. The politician who learns how to address the only child could induce a response that may create the support he/she desires.

A reason for learning to communicate with onlies is that they tend to react rather than interact. Simply talking at them can produce as much opposition as support. To communicate with the only child, the politician must refer to the thoughts, feelings and attitudes of the only child before making his/her points. The one who does this best has the best chance of persuading onlies.

Of course, the politician who communicates in the language of every birth order is going to reach the greatest number of people with his/her message. More people will probably vote for the person whom they feel shows he/she understands them by the way he/she communicates.

CONCLUSION

Birth order theory is still in its infancy, but promises to grow as we use it. As we use the concepts, we will keep on adding to our knowledge of our own behavior and that of others. The task before us calls us to think about what we observe, use the discoveries for our own growth and organize the knowledge to make it available for everyone.

— INDEX —